TRUE ADVENTURES

BOOKS BY DAN GREENBURG

How to Avoid Love and Marriage (with Suzanne O'Malley)

What Do Women Want?

Love Kills

Something's There

Scoring

Porno-graphics

Philly

Jumbo the Boy and Arnold the Elephant

Chewsday

How to Make Yourself Miserable

Kiss My Firm But Pliant Lips

How to Be a Jewish Mother

TRUE ADVENTURES

by DAN GREENBURG

FREUNDLICH BOOKS   New York

Copyright © Dan Greenburg 1985

Library of Congress Cataloging in Publication Data
Greenburg, Dan.
True adventures.
I Title.
PS3557.R379T7   1985   814'.54   85-1517
ISBN 0-88191-023-6 (pbk.)

Published by Freundlich Books
(A Division of Lawrence S. Freundlich Publications, Inc.)
80 Madison Avenue
New York, New York 10016

Distributed to the Trade by The Scribner Book Companies, Inc.

Manufactured in the United States of America

10 9 8 7 6 5 4 3 2 1

The author is grateful to the original publishers of his material
for their permission to reprint it here:

"Electricians," reprinted with the permission of *New York*
Magazine.

"Firefighters," reprinted with the permission of *LIFE* Magazine.

"Orgies," originally appeared in *Playboy* Magazine: Copyright ©
1972 by *Playboy*.

"Black Magic," reprinted with the permission of *Esquire*
Magazine.

"The Morgue," excerpted from *Love Kills*, copyright © 1978 by
Dan Greenburg. Reprinted by permission of Harcourt Brace
Jovanovich, Inc.

"Sex Ads," originally appeared in *Playboy* Magazine: Copyright
© 1976 by *Playboy*.

"Vengeance," reprinted with the permission of *Esquire* Magazine.

"Sandstone," originally appeared in *Playboy* Magazine: Copyright
© 1977 by *Playboy*.

"EST," originally appeared in *Playboy* Magazine: Copyright ©
1976 by *Playboy*.

For Naomi, Lee, Jonny and Joel

WHAT the ten experiences in this book have in common is this: They all really happened to me, and they were all threatening, either physically or psychically.

What you have to know about me up front is that I'm a coward. There is nothing in my life, no matter how benign or banal, whose contemplation cannot, if I'm given sufficient time to brood about it, fill me with dread. I am not just talking here about going to Haiti and taking part in voodoo ceremonies, or going to the South Bronx and running into burning buildings with firemen, or going to Scotland and getting involved in black magic, or going to Los Angeles and participating in orgies. I am also talking about going to a cocktail party or making a phone call or getting out of bed in the morning, because those have scared me too.

In trying to overcome my cowardice, I became counter-phobic—I overcompensated by deliberately seeking out frightening situations and thrusting myself into them to see if I could get rid of my fears. I also noticed an odd benefit of such experiences: The more frightened I was in a given situation, the more humorously I could write about it. "Bad for me, good for the piece," I continually found myself saying during my often dangerous research.

Not all of the pieces in this collection are funny, of course—the one on firefighters is not funny at all, and neither is the one on the morgue—but I am primarily a humorist, and so I hope you'll think that the other eight have at least some amusing moments.

The ten pieces in this collection were written between 1969 and 1977 and appeared in *Playboy, Esquire, Life,* and *New York* Magazine. They were selected from about three dozen I have written in this vein. I am today, in 1984, certainly not the man I was at the start of these pieces, but neither am I precisely the one I was at the end. I did overcome a profound fear of fire by riding with firefighters for five months—so much so that when a short circuit in an electrical outlet caused my bed to catch fire recently, I didn't run from the building as I might have before, I simply tore the mattress apart with my bare hands and beat out the flames. And I did overcome an almost terminal shyness about sex by hanging out at a Los Angeles sex club—so much so that toward the end, I was able to walk into a room of naked people making love to one another and join them without even *thinking* of throwing up. But the three sexual adventures were written at the end of a bad marriage and during my subsequent four years of bachelorhood, and today they seem a little breathless to me because I am happily remarried and no longer on the prowl.

Because these pieces were written between 1969 and 1977, some of the statistics quoted in them are no longer accurate; any price or wage mentioned, for example, you could safely double or triple and you'd be close to today's equivalent.

After all these qualifying remarks and excuses, I should

add that I'm very proud of the work. A couple of these pieces won me humor awards, and a third made me an honorary fire chief and a member of the International Association of Fire Fighters. I hope you like them too.

—DAN GREENBURG
New York City
January 1985

TRUE ADVENTURES

ELECTRICIANS

EARLY in May, shortly after we moved into our apartment, I bought an air conditioning unit big enough to cool our double-height living room and sleeping balcony. The unit cost $400,* and the installation fee—since the unit had to be mounted near the ceiling, at the top of our tall, double-height windows—was an additional $125.

The high installation fee was as much a surprise to me as the high cost of the air conditioner had been, but my surprises were far from over, as I began to realize once I handed the installer his check.

"I guess you know the wiring in this place isn't gonna handle that big of a cooling unit," he said.

"What?" I said.

"Your wiring," he said. "You're gonna need a heavy-duty line run in from the cooling unit to the circuit-breaker box back there."

"I see," I said. "How come you didn't take care of that when you installed the unit?"

* These are 1967 prices.

"Because I'm an installer, he said. "I don't do that kind of work."

"Oh?" I said. "Who does?"

"Any electrician," he said.

As a purely theoretical reply, I suppose this was valid enough. As a piece of practical information, saying that any electrician in New York will run a line and connect your air conditioner is, I have since learned, about as useful as saying that any boy in America can grow up to be the President—so few ever really manage to pull it off. It's not that electricians in New York are hostile or dishonest or anything like that. It's just that they don't appear to need the work. This reticence to serve (which is a characteristic of New York service people in general—automotive mechanics, TV repairmen, supers, cabdrivers, etc.) leads me to suspect that all these people have independent sources of income and are only working as a hobby.

As yet only dimly aware of this reticence in electricians, I set out to find one to hook up my air conditioner. I telephoned the man who does most of my landlady's electrical work, asked him when he'd be able to do the job and what it might cost. With a thick but unidentifiable accent, he said that he probably wouldn't be able to get to it for a couple of weeks and it would cost $75. I wasn't anxious to wait that long, and I thought $75 a bit high for merely putting in a glorified extension cord, so I thanked him and said I'd look elsewhere.

I phoned several electricians that day and told them my problem, but none seemed interested enough to even come by and give me an estimate.

The following day my wife was walking past a shop on First Avenue that sold air conditioners, so she stopped in and asked them what they'd charge to run a line for us. Their *official* price, said the helpful salesman she talked to, would probably run close to $60, but if one of the men did it on his own after work it would run considerably less—maybe as low as $40. This was more like it. Would the person who did the work be a licensed electrician? The salesman realized he was dealing with a child. *All* their men were licensed electricians, madam, he said. That evening about five the bell rang. When I opened the door and saw who it was, I didn't know how to act at first, because even though he was wearing green work clothes and even though he was using a different foreign accent than the one he used in *The Russians Are Coming, The Russians Are Coming*, the man at my door was clearly Alan Arkin.

"Good evening, sor," he said, "I am from de hairconditioner."

"The hairconditioner," I said. "I see."

I figured it was a Candid Camera stunt.

"Ees hokay eef I see heem, please?"

"Who?"

"De hairconditioner."

I saw no reason to spoil the stunt. I decided to play along. I invited him inside, showed him the air conditioner and the circuit-breaker box, and tried my best to answer his questions with a straight face.

He took a lot of measurements, muttering and chanting softly under his breath, and then he announced he'd return the following afternoon at four-thirty. The job would cost $40 and would be done in "habout a hour, geev or take." I kept waiting for him to reveal his true identity, but he didn't, so I figured I'd play it cool—if Candid Camera wanted Alan Arkin to connect my air conditioner, I certainly wasn't going to stop them.

The following afternoon at about five, he reappeared with tools and wire and conduit pipe and went noisily to work. I stood upstairs on the sleeping balcony and watched him drill holes into the railing and the floor and through the wall. By seven the balcony and the living room below it were littered with sawdust, bits of wire, pieces of plastic, and small chunks of wood that had broken off the balcony railing by accident, and it finally became clear to me that it wasn't Alan Arkin at all but his doppelganger who was ruining my apartment.

I pointed out as tactfully as I could that he'd originally estimated the work would take an hour, that it had already taken more than two, and that we had dinner guests arriving at eight. He assured me he was nearly finished. "Jaust a few smoll theengs and den he's raddy," he said. I excused myself and went to shower and shave and dress for dinner.

At eight our guests arrived. The electrician waved down to them from the balcony in solemn greeting and assured me he was just seconds away from completion: "Only jaust to dreel de holes to let heem breathe," was how I believe the technical explanation went.

We and our guests sat down and tried to speak above the whining of the electric drill, periodically brushing the fine rain of sawdust off our shoulders and picking the larger pieces out of our drinks.

At nine we got another reassuring pronouncement from the balcony, and then again at nine-thirty, and though we were all anxious to begin dinner, it seemed wisest to wait.

At ten, like some Eurasian monarch addressing his subjects, he signaled an end to all discussion and announced with evident pride that he was finished. "And now," he said dramatically, "I make heem work."

With a flourish he flipped the switch on the air conditioner. There was a crackle of electricity, a blinding white flash, and an anguished cry from above. I raced upstairs to the balcony to find the electrician sprawled, terrified, on the floor.

"I could have been *keelled*," he said in awe. "I could have been *keelled*."

I asked him if he was all right. He seemed unsure and absently patted his body for missing parts. At length he pulled himself together and explained that what had happened was that he'd accidentally shorted out the air conditioner by brushing his pliers against both the metal conduit pipe and the metal cover of the circuit-breaker box at the same time, and that although it was true he could have been keelled, he wasn't, and that everything would be all right with the air conditioner in the future if I just remembered not to brush my pliers against the conduit pipe and the circuit-breaker box cover at the same time.

The air conditioner itself was undamaged. But the refrigerator and the electric stove and half our lights were not. The electrician explained that the short-circuit had blown a fuse. I asked how that could be, since we didn't even *have* fuses, we had a circuit-breaker box. He explained that he meant the master fuse in the basement.

We went down to the basement to see if he was right. After peering about among the gas meters with a succession of lighted matches, which promised bigger and better blinding flashes, he finally found our master fuse. He'd been right. It was blown.

"Well," I said, "now we're really dead. Where are we going to get a master fuse at this time of night?"

"Easy," he said and gave me a terrific wink. "We sweetch heem weeth somebody's else."

I didn't understand at first, and then, unfortunately, I did.

"You mean you're going to take one of the other tenants' master fuses and switch it with ours?" I said.

He nodded.

"But you're turning off someone's electricity," I said.

He nodded again, relieved that I understood.

"But that's not ethical," I said.

He looked at me blankly.

"You don't weesh to sweetch heem weeth somebody's else?" he said.

"Well," I said, "it's just that it doesn't seem very neighborly or fair to shut off the better part of a guy's electricity like that, that's all."

The electrician shrugged philosophically.

"Either somebody *else* be weethout electreeceety tonight or else *you* be. Wheech you like batter?"

I thought briefly about our hungry, sawdust-sprinkled dinner guests upstairs, about our non-functioning stove and refrigerator, about how our newspaper was often swiped from in front of our door. Finally I shrugged and smiled the dark, embarrassed smile of one who has just discovered the extent of his own corruption.

The electrician nodded seriously in recognition of what had just taken place.

"Good," he said, welcoming me to the ranks of the morally bankrupt. "Who you weesh to sweetch heem weeth?"

I was not prepared for this. Faced with a moral crisis of such a magnitude, I did what any other New Yorker would have done: I turned my back and let the decision be made without me.

The rotten deed accomplished, we went back upstairs. The refrigerator, the stove, and the lights were once more working. The job, said the electrician, was now complete. I suppose I didn't look convinced, so he reached for the switch next to the air conditioner and, as we all cringed, he turned it on. Miraculously, it worked. No blinding flash, no anguished cry. Just a quietly humming motor and nice cool air.

The electrician smiled proudly and said that, seeing as how it was nearly eleven, he'd better be on his way home. I asked what I owed him—$40, as we'd agreed? He looked incredibly hurt—after all, it had taken him so much longer than he'd thought, and he *had* nearly been keeled.

How much did he feel that the job was worth—$45? $50 $55? When I got to $60 he shrugged and smiled and I began to write out the check. I asked him his name. He told me, and I wrote it on the check, and I know you will have a hard time believing me, but as God is my witness, the man was of the Arabic persuasion.

THE following day the air conditioner appeared to be performing normally, but I happened to lightly graze the conduit pipe with my hand and I received a small tingling shock. I couldn't believe it, so I touched the conduit pipe again, and again I received the shock. I pointed out this oddity to a friend who was visiting, and he volunteered the information that the air conditioner was not grounded and could, under the right conditions, rather efficiently electrocute us. An image of the electrician's face took shape in my mind, and with it a fantasy of Arab saboteurs prowling silently through the city, posing as electricians and boobytrapping all Zionist air conditioners.

I called the store where my Arabic friend worked and asked to speak to him. He was out on a job, they said (another Zionist had apparently been located), but he'd be back in about an hour.

"Listen," I said, "I know this is going to sound silly, but I'm going to ask you anyway, just to reassure myself. Do you happen to know for an absolute fact that the guy who hooked up my air conditioner is a licensed electrician?"

"A licensed electrician?" he said. Clearly, he was talking to a moron. "We sell and install air conditioners," he said. "Nobody here is a licensed electrician."

"I see," I said. Not knowing what else to do, I left a request that the unlicensed electrician come by after work and reevaluate his freelance creation.

In the meantime I decided that the easiest way to determine whether a horrible death by electrocution was in the cards was to call up a city building inspector and have him take a look at my wiring. I dialed the number of the proper municipal office and told the woman who answered what I wanted.

"Well, we *could* send out an inspector to look at your wiring," she said, "but I'm sure there's nothing to worry about. Provided the work was done by a licensed electrician, of course."

"Uh, well, what if it wasn't?" I said.

"Using unlicensed electricians is illegal," she said. "You'd probably be arrested."

"Arrested! But we thought he *was* licensed. They said at the store he was licensed."

"Doesn't matter," she said, adding automatically: "Ignorance of the law is no—"

"I know, I know. Listen, I don't want to be arrested. Isn't there anything else I can do?"

"Sure," she said. "Don't ask us to send out an inspector."

"Let me get this straight," I said. "The only way I can be sure whether my air conditioner isn't safe is to have an inspector come over here and check it. But if he comes over here and checks it and it isn't safe, I'll be arrested. And the only way I can be sure I won't be arrested is if I don't have the inspector come over here. Is that it?"

"That's it," she said.

"That's Catch-22," I said.

THAT evening after work the Arab showed up at our apartment. He went upstairs to the sleeping balcony, he touched the conduit pipe, he felt what I had felt, and he smiled philosophically. He knew what was wrong, of course, and was vastly amused he'd overlooked whatever it was he'd overlooked. He set to work, chuckling.

But the next day I again touched the conduit pipe and again received a shock, and I realized that further Arab-Zionist negotiations were not the answer.

I telephoned a few more electricians and found unanimous apathy toward my problem. The air conditioning season had begun in earnest, and they could afford to be even more picky about their patients than free psychoanalytic clinics. Our case, it seemed, did not intrigue them.

With pride in pocket, I called the house electrician and admitted I was now resigned to paying him the $75. When could he come and do the job?

"Well," he said in his unidentifiable accent, "I preety beesy now, baut eef I een de building anyhow, den porhops een a week or two I do eet."

"In a week?" I said wistfully.

"Porhops a week. Porhops leetle more."

"How much more?"

"Well, porhops *not* more den a week—porhops even less."

"Less?"

"Porhops less, yes. Baut porhops more, also."

"Well, let's try to be specific here. How about a week from today?"

"What ees today?"

"Thursday. How about a week from Thursday?"

"Week from Torsday? Well, det might be hokay. Porhops I even do eet sooner, though."

"Oh?"

"Yes, porhops I do eet Wansday."

"Wednesday?"

"Yes. Wansday be hokay?"

"Sure. Wednesday's fine."

"Porhops I even be able make eet Toosday."

"Well, that's even better. Which day shall we make it then, Wednesday or Tuesday?"

"Well, I daun't know. Porhops I naut be able to do eet soon as det after all. Porhops I naut be able gat to eet unteel Torsday after all."

"That's perfectly all right. Shall we say next Thursday then for sure?"

"Well, I theenk so. Onless I could to do eet sooner."

"Fine. Great. Thursday it is, then."

"Porhops you batter call me, though, een case I naut be able to make eet."

"O.K., when should I call you?"

"Call me Maunday about seex-feefteen."

"Great. Monday, six-fifteen it is."

"No. Porhops eenstead you call me Toosday."

"Tuesday?"

"Toosday. No, I daun't know eef I be home Toosday. Porhops eenstead you call me Wansday."

I hung up. He was either toying with me or else he was a mental defective. I wasn't thrilled with either possibility.

It was at this point that our doorbell decided to give out. It just began ringing one day and wouldn't stop. The super was persuaded to come over and have a look at it. He unscrewed the faceplate from the doorbell, peered at the insides of it and shrugged. "There's nothin' *I* can do with this," he said, as it continued to ring.

"Can't you even stop the ringing?" I said.

He stuck his hand inside the wall and ripped out all the wires. The ringing stopped.

"What about putting it back together now so it works?" I said.

"I don't do that kind of work," he said.

"Oh," I said. "Who does?"

"Any electrician," he said.

I placed more phone calls. I now had two jobs to offer— an air conditioner *and* a doorbell—but still none of the electricians I spoke to felt our case was interesting enough to even take a look.

Before long it was the beginning of July. We had been without an air conditioner for nine weeks and a doorbell for nearly eight. To get into our lobby, friends and messengers and delivery boys either rang our neighbors' doorbells and explained to them that the Greenburgs' bell was broken, or else they just went woundedly away and were never heard from again. Our neighbors gave us chilly stares when we passed them in the halls. We didn't dare to use our air conditioner.

And then one day I had an idea: I would ask the only friendly, reliable businessman in the neighborhood if he could give me the name of an electrician with a heart. He *could*— he knew an excellent man in the Bronx who had once put in an air conditioner for *him*.

My pulse racing wildly, I called the electrician in the Bronx. I told him of my plight. Not only was he sympathetic, not only did he promise to come over the very next day at ten a.m., he was also literate, charming, genuinely witty, and he spoke perfect English. I considered inviting him to dinner. Clearly, our troubles were as good as over.

The next day, to my great amazement, my sympathetic, literate, charming, witty friend stood me up. I telephoned to find out why. He was terribly apologetic and charming and he promised faithfully to come over the following afternoon at one. I hung up. I waited. He never showed.

I called him again and he was even more apologetic and charming than the time before. Emergency calls had come in at the last moment on both occasions, he said, but since he had treated me so shamefully he was coming over the next day at noon, even if he had to be carried on a stretcher.

I don't know why I was surprised when he didn't show up the third time, but I was. I called him up and asked if it had been another emergency. Yes, that was it, he said, another emergency. And he just felt rotten about the whole thing, he really did—he didn't blame me if I never spoke to him again.

"Well," I said wearily, "why don't you just pick a time when you don't think you'll be too busy? It doesn't even have to be tomorrow, it doesn't even have to be this week, just so long as you can assure me I can count on you."

"Well, that's just it," he said, "I'm afraid you *can't* count on me."

"Pardon me?"

"I said I'm afraid you can't ever count on me. Frankly, Mr. Greenburg, I'm not very reliable."

Aging rapidly, I stared at a blank spot on the wall and tried to pretend I hadn't heard what I'd just heard. It had been well over ten weeks by now and I was getting very tired of the whole thing, and besides I didn't think I could cope with electricians who told you that frankly they weren't very reliable. Somehow I was beginning to feel the kind of shabby feeling you get at the end of a bad love affair, so I did what you sometimes did when you found yourself in one of those when you were young: I asked the electrician if he had a nice friend.

"Well," he said, "I *could* give you the name of a man I know in Brooklyn who does this kind of work. But frankly, Mr. Greenburg, he won't come either."

"He won't?" I said dully. "Why not?" Whenever you thought you had reached the absolute nadir in demeaning situations, you always found there was still a little lower you could sink.

"Let me give you some advice, Mr. Greenburg."

"Yeah."

"The next electrician you call, don't tell him about your doorbell."

"My doorbell."

"Tell him about your air conditioner, but don't tell him about your doorbell. Electricians hate doorbells. I, personally, happen to be an *expert* on doorbells, and even *I* won't touch them."

I hung up, thoroughly humiliated.

That afternoon my wife and I took out the Yellow Pages and systematically called every electrician in Manhattan. When we finished we had made appointments with thirteen of them. Only one of these men ever showed up. The rest didn't even call to cancel. The man who did show up fixed our doorbell in five minutes and our air conditioner (for $75) in less than an hour.

It had taken twelve weeks, $260, and some eighty to ninety man-hours on the telephone, we had been morally bankrupted and personally degraded, but we finally got the job done.

With New York electricians, as with Presidential candidates, many are called, few are chosen. And one, if you're lucky, shows up to do the job.

FIREFIGHTERS

I HAVE always been terrified of fire. I've never been caught in a bad fire, and I've never known anyone who was, so I don't know where this terror of mine comes from. I do remember that when I was a little boy in Chicago, there was an awful fire caused by the collision of a streetcar and an oil truck in which scores of streetcar passengers were trapped and burned to death. The newspapers for days featured photographs of hideously charred bodies that I could neither bear to look at nor manage not to, and those pictures have ever since typified the horror of fire to me. But that was not the cause of a traumatic reaction to fire, merely a manifestation of it.

Now, as an adult, about once a week I awake at some dark hour before dawn thinking that I smell smoke. With the long ago image of those burnt bodies flickering inside my head, I creep out of bed, grab my flashlight, and go prowling around the apartment, poking the beam into corners, sniffing about for wisps of smoke, inhaling so deeply I nearly pass out from hyperventilation. And then, satisfied that the holocaust has not yet come, I return to bed, taking care to place my trousers and boots right near me on the floor, fireman fashion, in case I should need them in a hurry.

A few months ago my wife and I were lying asleep in the early evening, and from somewhere came the sound of sirens. Closer and closer they came, until dawned my realization that they had stopped in front of our building. I was already into my pants as the doorbell rang. Heart hammering in my ears, I raced to the door, as my wife ran madly about, corralling our cats for the imminent exodus. I opened the door and met three of the largest men in the world, wearing black helmets, black rubber coats and boots, carrying axes and long steel tools with hooks at the ends.

As it happened, the fire that night was not in our recently purchased co-op apartment but in the one below us, and it was a very tiny fire at that. But before the firemen climbed back on their trucks I overheard one of them remark that our newly renovated building was, in his opinion, little short of a firetrap.

That experience triggered many urgent questions in me, not only about the wisdom of having gone into hock up to my eyeballs for the privilege of living in a luxury firetrap, but also about what exactly *does* go on in a fire, what precisely *should* you do if ever caught in one, and why anyone in his right mind would ever fight fires for a living.

My knowledge about firemen, I realized, came largely from children's books and had to do with smiling men in blue who rescued pussycats from trees and with friendly dalmatians who led toddlers in Dr. Denton's through smoke to safety and with gutsy little red fire engines who chatted anthropomorphically away with their drivers. The real story, I felt, was probably somewhat different, especially in a place like New York, where among other things, slum folks lob cans and bottles at firemen from their windows.

I decided to find out what the real story was.

.   .   .

I BEGAN my investigation at our neighborhood firehouse on East 51st Street which is, at least physically, a fairly typical firehouse. It contains an engine or "pumper," a hook-and-ladder truck, and a chief's car. The decor, as in most city firehouses, is Early Institutional: grimy cream-colored tiles and blechy green paint on the walls, worn gray cement floors, industrial fluorescent fixtures, and exposed plumbing and wiring overhead. The fire vehicles, in sharp contrast to their grim surroundings, stand shiny red and chromed and exquisitely maintained, with neat piles of helmets, folded rubber "turnout" coats, and boots at each man's assigned station on the truck. The clothes are dingy and worn and reek of smoke and fires past.

I lean against a fire truck, interviewing my first fireman, when suddenly the alarm bells begin tapping in. All conversation ceases as the men silently begin counting the taps (firemen automatically count *any* bells they hear, even those in department stores), and then they know the signal is one of theirs. "Everyone goes, everyone goes!" shouts the man assigned to dispatch either truck, engine, chief's car, or any combination thereof, and the firehouse explodes into activity: men dashing for their stations, jumping into boots and coats and leaping onto the trucks, powerful engines starting up, firehouse doors rolling open—and someone who doesn't know I haven't yet been cleared to ride in anything but the chief's car yells at me to hop aboard the hook-and-ladder truck, and I do. Within seconds we are speeding across 51st Street on a fire truck as long as a five-story building is high—lights flashing, sirens screaming close to the threshold of pain, diesel-train air horns almost drowning out the sirens, tearing around corners and through stoplights and around slow moving traffic and cabs that refuse to get out of our way, riding in the left lane against oncoming cars, and as I hang onto the side of the truck, I know that any second now we are going to have a grinding head-on collision and I'm not the slightest bit concerned. After all, it's *fire* I'm afraid of, not traffic accidents.

As we slow down at the fire site, we are joined by more vehicles from other firehouses—three engines, two trucks, and a chief's car are assigned to most alarms in the city. The men leap off my truck and are gone so swiftly I don't even see them disappear. It's only later I will learn that the irons man has taken his forcible-entry tools and the can man his extinguisher and they've entered the building with the ladder company officer to search for people and fire, that the roof man has somehow reached the roof to "vent" it—to release the trapped smoke and heat which make firefighting most dangerous, while outside the engine company is connecting hoses to hydrants and preparing to extinguish the blaze.

As swiftly as they disappeared, they've returned. "Food on the stove," says someone with evident irritation—firemen hate little cooking fires, rubbish fires and car fires almost as much as false alarms—and then we are all back on the truck again and speeding back to the firehouse.

"You know what the super of that building said as we started to go in there?" says the man hanging on next to me.

"What?"

"Told us to use the service entrance because he'd just shined up all the brass in the lobby."

NEW YORK's fire department responds to more fire alarms in a single day than Boston's does in a week or Denver's does in a month. New York's fire department responds to more fires in a year than do the fire departments of Chicago, Los Angeles, Detroit, and Philadelphia combined. New York has not only the biggest and busiest fire department, it also has the best trained. And yet the New York Fire Department's equipment is so old and out-of-date it staggers the mind.

The coats firemen wear do not pass even the minimum flammability requirements for children's sleepwear. The hoses they carry into burning buildings weigh fifty-five pounds per folded-up section and are made of flammable cotton. In at least one company I know of in New York, they still use wooden ladders. The bulky air masks firemen use weigh thirty pounds and were developed during World War II. Their heavy leather helmets and the rest of their uniforms were designed over a hundred years ago.

With this ancient equipment they fight fires in so-called fireproof buildings where they must carry their ninety pounds of equipment up twenty to thirty flights of stairs, because the first thing that happens at a fire in one of these buildings is that the elevators stop working. The second thing that happens is that the interior becomes an oven, at temperatures up to 1,200 to 1,500° F., because the windows weren't designed to open and so the heat and smoke and gasses inside build up pressure until they blow out the walls. Even if firemen could manage to smash the glass of these unopenable windows with their axes (the glass is about one and one-half inches thick), they don't dare to because glass flying from those heights tends to travel about a block and decapitate whomever it hits at street level. The furniture in these buildings is usually made of polyurethane foam, which has been found to be as flammable as jet fuel. It's been said that it takes no more than an angry cockroach gnashing its teeth to ignite polyurethane foam. Once ignited it gives off a toxic gas that can kill you. Sometimes it explodes. (The Apollo I blaze that killed three astronauts was attributed to polyurethane foam.)

Robert Powers, Superintendent of the New York Board of Fire Underwriters, says, "The term *fire-resistive* as applied to the newer type of buildings is a misnomer. These buildings should be more properly called *semicombustible*."

. . .

Max Siegel, Al Soto, and Dan Nastro are members of Ladder 2, or 2 Truck, in the 51st Street firehouse. There are eight people in Manhattan who are alive today because on December 4, 1970, Siegel and Soto and Nastro went into a new fireproof building at 919 Third Avenue and pulled them out before they died. Pulling them out entailed crawling through a maze of hallways so choked with smoke that Nastro's portable searchlight was useless, so hot that steel beams were buckling and concrete was crumbling all around them. Siegel, Soto, and Nastro somehow made those rescues without air masks too—it takes thirty to sixty seconds to strap on an air mask, and sometimes that's the difference between rescuing a live person and a corpse. All these men won rescue medals, along with cash awards of $200 each; they spent the money the night of the awards ceremony taking all the off-duty guys in the firehouse out for dinner.

The New York Fire Department awards three classes of medals for rescues. I asked a fireman if he could give me an example of a typical rescue for each class of medal.

"Let's put it this way," he said. "You wake up one night and your bedroom is in flames. I come in and pull you out of there, O.K.?"

"O.K., I said.

"That's not even a rescue," he said. "That's routine. That's part of the regular job."

"Tell me about someone who won a specific class of medal," I said.

"O.K. This guy Gudelis, a lieutenant in Thirteen Truck, had just come back from a good fire where he'd made a pretty good rescue, and half an hour later he's at another fire making his search of the building before the engine has water in its lines, and he's almost literally blown out of there by flames and heat. He crawls in a second time and again he's blown out of there, only now he's sustained second-degree burns on his hands and knees. But he thinks he's heard a woman moaning inside, so he crawls back in on his second-degree burns and sure enough he finds an elderly woman and drags her out of there in time to save her life. He wanted to go back in a fourth time to look for more people, but the chief forced him into an ambulance. Gudelis got a second-class medal for that rescue."

"Only second-class?" I said. "What do you have to do to get a *first*-class medal?"

"For a first-class medal," he said, "you practically have to die."

It's interesting to note that of thirty rescue medals awarded to New York firemen last June, four were earned by men who were off-duty at the time of the rescue.

I tend to talk a lot about firemen these days. Not long ago I was at a cocktail party, and the woman I was talking to stopped me with a patronizing smile. "What is this hang-up firemen have about saving people?" she said.

I no longer remember the woman's name or face, but her words still hang in my head: *What is this hang-up firemen have about saving people?* Incredible. What is the hang-up we have about supposing that firemen's eagerness to save people is a hang-up? Clearly, firefighting has become as much of an anachronism as bullfighting—which, in its appeal to fierce working-class male pride and heroism, it somewhat resembles. Firefighters' uniforms and equipment are as outmoded today as their bravery. They are the last heroes left in a society that no longer understands heroes, a society so sophisticated and so cynical that heroes have become something of an embarrassment. If you don't think so, ride with them, as I have, in good neighborhoods and hear the sheepish and self-conscious things people say to them there. Or better yet, ride with them, as I have, in *bad* neighborhoods and hear what hostile and vicious things people say to them *there*. Or *do* to them there.

In places like Brownsville or the South Bronx, I'd heard

that folks tend to peg the random bottle at passing fire trucks. What I hadn't heard till I got there is that folks also tend to ease the random couch or Frigidaire off the roof to fall on firemen's heads. And jump hose men and beat them bloody. And slash their hoses. And raid the firehouse while the men are at fires, and steal their TV and their clothes, and kill firehouse pets. And booby-trap abandoned buildings by cutting holes in floors, sawing through stairways, and taking the bolts out of fire escapes before setting the structures on fire. Here are two particularly grisly tricks slum arsonists play on firemen: One is to fill up little sandwich-size Baggies with gasoline and tack them to the ceiling before lighting the fire. The second is to wait till the firemen have thrown enough water on the fire so they're sloshing around in it up to their ankles, then to float a few gallons of gas on top of the water and light it. Then, of course, you also have your rifles. Firemen are shot at so frequently by snipers that there's an official fire department regulation covering the situation. The regulation states that if a company finds they're being shot at they are permitted to fight the fire from the rear of the building and the corners, rather than the front. "This," said one chief dryly, "is based on the concept that a man with a rifle is unable to turn around and shoot the other way."

Why would anybody *do* such things, particularly to firemen?

"Because they're a bunch of vicious bastards, that's why," said a chief who's spent some twenty years in Brownsville.

"What do you mean?" I said, my liberal Jewish back arched.

"I mean that you go and pull someone out of a fire who's unconscious and badly burned and you give him mouth-to-mouth resuscitation—you're not thinking about what color he is, you're trying to save his life. And he's puking in your mouth because that's what fire victims do, and you spit out the puke and continue giving him mouth-to-mouth till he starts breathing again. And the next time you go back there that same guy is just as likely as not one of those who's throwing rocks at you."

Less emotional answers go as follows: that there is a fairly low percentage of blacks in the fire department; that firemen, like policemen, are not thought to be sympathetic to the black community; that ghetto people don't understand why firemen pull down their ceilings and walls after the fire is out (the firemen are looking for "extensions"—fire that smolders inside walls and creeps along to break out later); that firemen are unarmed and make pretty good targets; that firemen are the only members of the white establishment that most ghetto people see on a regular basis. (As a matter of fact ghetto people do call firemen for muggings, stabbings, rapes, murders, overdoses of drugs, delivery of babies. Why? "You're the only ones who come when we call for help," firemen are told.)

ONE NIGHT an officer in the 51st Street firehouse said to me: "You know, you're not going to do either you or us any good just standing across the street at fires, taking notes. Why don't you come in with us and find out what it's really like in there?" I was both flattered and frightened, but I agreed. Through a lot of finagling downtown, and by signing in triplicate a notarized statement to the effect that neither I nor my widow would have any beef coming if I got killed or maimed in one of their fires, I finally secured permission to ride on fire trucks and enter burning buildings. I also got the long-term loan of an actual firemen's helmet, coat, and boots.

I looked absurd in my uniform, but I didn't care. I put it on every night before walking to the 51st Street firehouse. The firemen eyed me warily and told me it'd be perfectly O.K. to leave my gear with them. I told them I needed it at home because the boys downtown had agreed to pick me up there and take me to all major fires. While this was not untrue, the real reason I wanted my gear at home was that I loved it.

As I put on my uniform and prepared to walk to the firehouse one night, I noticed it was raining rather heavily—too heavily to walk the three blocks to the firehouse without an umbrella. Unfortunately, the only one left in our closet was a multicolored golf umbrella with jolly stripes and peppy polka dots. I knew how goofy I'd look carrying it, but it was raining too hard for me to bother about appearances.

When I was halfway there, I heard sirens start up. I walked back toward First Avenue and it seemed to me I saw flashing red lights a few blocks down. As I stood in the downpour waiting for the light to change, with my uniform and helmet and my perky umbrella, looking like a fireman who'd lost his truck, I became aware that the vehicle closest to me was a taxicab and that its driver was staring at me in undisguised fascination.

"Where's the fire, Sarge?" he said.

"I really don't know," I said.

It was clearly the kind of moment all New York cabdrivers live for. He turned to his passengers in the back. "He's a fireman, but he don't know where the fire is," he said. Explosive laughter from the audience. The cabbie turned back to me and, a sly smile playing about his lips, produced a pack of matches, lit one, and held it up to me.

"*Here's* the fire, Sarge," he said.

THE first time I heard the expression "a good fire" I asked what it meant and was answered defensively. That term didn't mean firemen like to see people hurt or property destroyed, I was told. It was just that some fires were a challenge and others, like little cooking fires and rubbish fires, were a waste of time. A captain who'd been around long enough to be relaxed with reporters finally gave me a direct and colorful answer. "A good fire?" he said. "Well, when you come tearing around the corner on the rig and you see flames roaring out of about six windows and people spilling out of a building—that's a good fire."

It would be easy to get the wrong impression about firemen just from listening to them talk. They have the gallows humor that's needed in any profession as grisly as theirs, and they do try to maintain a nice rough-and-tumble image too. I know a fireman who is about to receive his Ph.D. in psychology, another who's a poet, one who's a C.P.A., and one who used to be a concert violinist, and almost to a man they'd prefer to have you think they just stepped out of *F-Troop* or *The Dirty Dozen*. They'll tell you endless stories to maintain the image.

"The guys in this place are animals, absolute animals," says a captain fondly of his men. "*You've* seen the way they eat around here—you don't keep moving, they'll bite your arm. One time we had a very strict chief. Very strict. Insisted on keeping the food cabinet locked except at mealtime. The men took a fire axe and chopped the goddamned cabinet right off the wall." The captain chuckles at the memory. "You know one way they pass the time in a firehouse in a really rough neighborhood when there aren't any jobs coming in?"

"Tell me."

"They take a trash can full of greasy rags and lock themselves into the firehouse kitchen with it, they light it and create a smoke condition and then see which one of them can take it the longest." Another chuckle. "Well, you've got to realize that to do the kind of work that these guys do, especially in places like Brownsville or the South Bronx, requires their maintaining a very high level of nervous energy. So if you've got all this energy built up and there aren't any fires coming in to use it at—well, you've got to use it up *somehow*."

.   .   .

THREE TIMES as many firemen die in the line
of duty as policemen. A policeman gets shot and it's page one
news for days. A fireman dies every five weeks in a fire in New
York and we never even hear about it. A man cannot get into
the fire department unless his heart is in perfect condition,
yet once on the job firemen have 1,200 percent more heart
trouble than policemen. National Safety Council figures show
that firemen have the most dangerous job in the country—
they have three times as many injuries as the next most haz-
ardous profession, underground coal miners. Firemen live nine
years less than other men.

Why would anyone want to be a fireman? I asked a great
many firemen, and I got a great variety of answers, ranging
from the noble and altruistic to the needlessly self-effacing,
but the explanation that seems to cover the greatest number
of cases is a simple one. There are a sprinkling of Jewish
firemen and black ones and a great many Italian ones, but
the largest group of firemen by far are the Irish. And when
you were poor and Irish and growing up in New York a couple
of decades ago, the nuns never spoke about becoming a doctor
or a lawyer, they told you to become a cop or a fireman. Im-
migrant Irish and Italian parents felt that the only secure jobs
were in civil service, just as my own Depression-traumatized
Jewish parents in Chicago felt that the only secure jobs were
in teaching.

During the four months of the winter of 1971–72 while I
was researching this story, both cops and firemen made the
news. Cops because the Knapp Commission found out policemen were taking an awful lot of bribes. Firemen because the
city had let them work for over a year without negotiating a
new contract. Firemen aren't allowed to strike, of course, so
instead they tried a milder sort of job action: Every time a
fireman got injured in a fire he asked to see a doctor. Up to
then firemen had just kept quiet about minor burns or heat

exhaustion or massive smoke inhalation and simply gone on to the next fire—often without a chance to either rest up or to get some of the poisons from the fire out of their bodies. The press didn't understand the firemen's job action and dubbed it "the blue flu." Up till the job action, even firemen who'd been seriously disabled would plead to be allowed back to work before they were legally supposed to. But now they figured the hell with it. They figured if nobody gives a damn about us, what are we beating our brains out for? And that was really what their job action was about, even more than the increase in salary.

"It's not the goddamned money," says Nick Cavatero, who works for the firemen's union. "It's that they want to be loved —they used to be and now they aren't."

Well, the contract finally went through. And the cops got the same raise as the firemen, because cops in New York have a parity arrangement with firemen. Firemen say cops live three times as well as they do on the same salary because of bribes. Although garbage men theoretically get only 90 percent of what firemen do, they wind up with more at the end of the year due to overtime clauses. I read this sign on a firehouse bulletin board: "The man who collects your garbage makes more money than you do, he can retire on a higher pension than you do, *and* he lives longer than you do!"

Certain things haven't been changed by the new contracts, nor are they likely to be. Firemen still not only have to buy their own food while on the job, in most cases they have to buy the very stove they cook it on. They also have to buy their own dishwasher, firehouse TV set, their own paper towels for the restroom, their own bandages for the first-aid kit, and even their own halligan forcible-entry tools.

Firemen have always spent their own money trying to im-prove conditions in their decrepit firehouses and trying to update their ancient firefighting equipment. Lt. Bill Mc-Laughlin at 2 Truck showed me a new forcible-entry device he invented called a K-Tool, which enables firemen to open a locked door, with practically no damage to the door, in just thirty seconds. What Lt. McLaughlin neglected to mention was that he'd spent $4,000 of his own money having a number of K-Tools made and distributed to the fire companies in his division.

THE SOUTH BRONX. One of the most wretched and terrifying slums in the world. Packs of wild dogs roam the area at night. The grim streets are heaped with rotting garbage, decaying pieces of furniture, and hulks of rusted metal that were once shiny automobiles and are now nothing at all, having been stripped of engines, radios, tires, wheels, seats, chrome, anything removable, and set afire. Their burnt-out carcasses crouch at curbside or in the middle of the street. It's the night before Christmas Eve, and no signs of life can be seen either in the street or in the steel-shuttered, iron-gated buildings. Surviving structures alternate with skeletons of burnt-out buildings and vacant lots strewn with rubble of buildings that have burned literally to the ground. There are people living here somewhere, mainly blacks and Puerto Ricans, but they are apparently no more anxious to walk the streets than I am, and I am not at all.

The firehouse on 169th and Intervale is called "La Casa Grande"—the Big House—and it is the busiest firehouse in New York, if not the world. It houses 82 Engine and it's empty when I get there, except for a covering officer and a chief's car with its right front door torn off. The men will be back any minute now, the officer assures me.

Firemen in New York work two nine-hour day shifts, or "tours," are off two days, then work two fifteen-hour night tours and are off three days. Day tours are nine a.m. to six p.m., night tours six p.m. to nine a.m. Most fires occur between three p.m. and one a.m., so the night tours tend to be the lively ones. It's now eight-thirty p.m. and both 82 Engine and

31 Truck are out on a run—their tenth since they came on duty only two and one-half hours ago. Soon the large doors open wide, the truck and the engine back carefully inside, and the firemen stream in, shucking off boots and helmets and rubber coats, and piling them neatly at their stations.

I'm introduced to Dennis Smith, the man I'm going to be riding with tonight. He's the author of a powerful book about the life of a fireman, *Report from Engine Co. 82.* He is good-looking, smart, serious, soft-spoken. He arranges for me to share this evening's dinner, gets a bed for me to sleep on in the dorm upstairs and a seat next to him amidships on the engine, just as the bells tap in run number eleven of the evening. We slip into our coats and boots and helmets and jump aboard the engine as it revs up and tears out onto Intervale Avenue.

Fighting a fire in a tenement is not the same as fighting a fire in other buildings. For one thing, as you crawl down the hot, smoke-charged hallways on your belly, you often encounter hordes of rats and cockroaches coming the other way, swarming over you in their panic to flee the fire. As one fireman observed wryly to me, "It's not a natural thing to remain in a burning building."

Having decided to follow the men into fires tonight, I am relieved to learn as we slow down at the fire site that it's merely "food on the stove" and we're free to go.

Back at the firehouse, Dennis takes me into the long narrow dining room behind the apparatus floor, which is cheerily hung with Christmas decorations. A fireman named Walter Porr is telling me an incredible story about a crazed motorist who made four unsuccessful tries to run him down as he climbed off the fire truck the night before, as run number twelve taps in. Again we jump on the engine. A false alarm. We return to quarters.

The men begin their dinner. Huge portions of stuffed pork chops and vegetables and potatoes are handed around. As we dig into the hot tasty food, run number thirteen comes in. Dennis smiles at me and we run for the engine. Another false alarm. Back to dinner, which is no longer hot. But before we've taken more than a couple of mouthfuls we're off on run number fourteen. "You know," says Dennis wistfully, "for a period of around three months there I didn't have a single meal that wasn't interrupted by a run."

We pull up at the fire site, and from the crowd of people outside and the quantity of smoke, we know this is a real fire. Fighting back strong urgings to remain on the engine and hear about what happened afterward, I hotfoot it after Dennis and the others into the burning building. Neighbors tell us the fire was started by a man who'd had a fight with his wife. The lobby of the building is a scene of controlled chaos. Through thick smoke that makes my eyes sting, my nose run, and my throat burn, I can make out several firemen calmly leading dazed elderly or very young black people downstairs from the floors above and over the linguini of coiled flat hoses on the lobby floor, while a knot of perhaps ten firemen with long steel hooks and extinguishers and nozzles of as yet un-filled hoses crouches at the doorway of an apartment about twelve feet from where I'm standing. The apartment is cur-tained in flame.

Pushing down something odd which has begun to rise in my throat, I move up to the group of crouching firemen and take a position behind them like an umpire. Flames are now shooting out of the doorway over our heads, and all at once there is a loud report and a shower of sparks in our faces as the gas meter inside the apartment explodes. To my amaze-ment, the firemen in front of me now get up and walk right into the blazing room with their extinguishers as calmly as you or I would stroll into the kitchen for a Mallomars. The water from the hydrants outside finally fills the lines in the lobby and more firemen move into the blazing apartment.

Within two minutes more it is over. The flames are knocked

down, the fire is out. The air is hot and steamy and even smokier than before, and the truck men are now sticking their long hooks into ceilings and pulling them down, searching for extensions of fire, raining chunks of plaster and charred lath down on our heads. The engine men train their hoses on the remaining pockets of fire in the ceiling; then, leaving the "truckies" to finish their overhaul, they begin to "take up"— to drain and roll up their hoses and leave. Very soon indeed we are back on the engine, coughing and spitting and returning to our, by now, ice-cold pork chops. I am exhilarated, thinking I have finally seen a good fire, but one of the hose men sets me straight: "That was a ten-cent fire," he says.

Run number fifteen is an outside rubbish fire, run number sixteen a false alarm, run number seventeen a Christmas tree someone has set on fire in the hallway of an apartment building. "The old Christmas tree trick," a fireman says wryly.

I question Dennis about his job. He has been a fireman for nine years now, the last six of them at 82 Engine. During this time he has somehow managed to earn not only a bachelor's degree in English at night school, but also a master's, in addition to writing his book. Why, I ask, would someone as smart and sensitive as he obviously is want to be not only a fireman but a fireman in the busiest, most dangerous company in the city?

"It's a matter of pride," he says, "to be in the best outfit, the toughest one, with the best trained men on the job. Do you know there's a waiting list to get in here? I was in a slower company before I transferred here and I couldn't take it. I got bored." He pauses reflectively and smiles. "I guess it also has to do with being more of a man, with being more virile, with machismo and all the rest of it—I understand all that, but it doesn't make me want to do it any less."

Runs number eighteen through twenty-one are false alarms. But run number twenty-two is another real fire. As we approach the fire site we learn by radio that it's on an upper floor of a fireproof building. By the time we pull up at the site several men have already donned their cumbersome air masks. I tear after Dennis into the building. The fire is on the ninth floor. The men trot to the elevator. *The elevator!* If there's one thing I've learned at the 51st Street firehouse it's *never* to get into an elevator in a fireproof-building fire.

"What are you *doing!*" I yell like an imbecile to these seasoned veterans. "This thing is going to stop at the fire floor and incinerate us!"

"That's only if you're *above* the fire floor," Dennis explains patiently. "We're *below* it."

The elevator doors open and I see that the elevator itself is already partially filled with smoke.

"We're going to the eighth floor," says Dennis. "The fire's on the ninth. You don't have to come with us if you don't want to."

I get into the elevator. The doors close and I look around me. There are eight firemen and me packed into the small, smoky space. I can see tomorrow's headlines: 9 DEAD IN S. BRONX: 8 HEROES, 1 SCHMUCK. This is truly the stupidest thing I have ever done in my life, and I'm already engaged in heavy bargaining with God for years of gratitude in the rabbinate in exchange for only a light maiming instead of a horrible charbroiled death. I follow our painfully slow progress by the lit floor numbers overhead: . . . 2 . . . 3 . . . 4 . . . 5 . . . 6 . . . 7 . . . 8. The elevator shudders and stops. The doors open. Black smoke pours in on us. We get out. We have indeed stopped at the floor below the fire floor, and I am now committed to a life in the pulpit. The men walk upstairs to the fire floor. I follow them.

The smoke is considerably thicker in the stairwell of the fire floor. Several men disappear into the total blackness of the hallway off the stairwell, carrying forcible-entry tools and extinguishers. The others unhook hoses attached to the wall and turn the wheel that fills them with water. I am coughing and gagging impressively. The hose men also disappear into blackness and very soon the fire is out. Leaving through the lobby, we are heckled by residents of the building. The firemen appear not to hear them. We return to quarters.

Run number twenty-three is a car fire, run number twenty-four an oil-burner fire, run number twenty-five a false alarm. It is now four-thirty a.m. and we decide to try to get some sleep. We go upstairs to the dorm, take off our boots and trousers, climb under the gray wool blankets, and the lights go off in the immense bare room. Silence. "I want my teddie," says a voice in the darkness. "Santa is bringing teddies for all good firemen *tomorrow*," says another voice. I am back in summer camp. And loving it.

Suddenly the bells come tapping in, the lights snap on, and we are all out of bed and into our pants and boots and down the pole onto the engine exactly seventeen minutes after we'd climbed under the covers.

As we speed through the deserted city on run number twenty-six, it seems to me I am watching a Godard movie. I am beginning to know the neighborhood by now, and I realize with a kind of creepy awareness that cars which have stood wrecked and stripped on streets adjoining the firehouse on previous runs have disappeared and other ones have taken their places. Ten yards from the spot where I'd noticed the silhouette of a smashed Cadillac limousine there is now a gutted Corvette. We tear around one more corner and grind to a stop in front of an abandoned building whose entire top floor is in flames. We jump off the engine but the officer yells at us to get back on. *Our* fire is around the corner—*this* fire belongs to five other companies that are even now screeching to a stop alongside us. We go on to our own fire—another abandoned building, only this one's *bottom* floor is the one in flames. I stand a few feet away from the wall of fire, warming myself as at a wienie roast, while behind me the hose men hook up to the hydrant. Eventually this fire is out too.

We get back to the firehouse and go up to bed, and I know we aren't going to be up there very long. A few firemen, I notice, aren't bothering to go upstairs anymore and have slumped forward with eyes closed at their stations on the engine. It's about a half hour before the bells come in again and we lurch into our clothes and onto the engine. I'm feeling gummy and dizzy and barely more than half awake as we pull out for run number twenty-seven. Another false alarm. We return to bed and I really don't know how many more runs I'll be able to take.

When the bells tap in for run number twenty-eight and the lights come on in the dorm, I can't tell whether I've been asleep and had an awful dream or whether it's just the nightmarish images of flames and wrecked cars and burning buildings I've seen all night that are beginning to fuse together. It is all I can do to go through the motions of dressing and climbing down to the engine before it leaves. The sky is beginning to get light, and as we approach the site, word comes over the radio that it's a fire in an occupied dwelling and it looks bad.

We draw up in front of the building and smoke is pouring out of the ground floor toward the rear, and as we charge back to where the fire is, it looks very bad indeed. Several of the men, some with air masks and some without, smash their way in through the windows, and by now a small crowd has gathered and there is talk of a child trapped inside. Hoses are pushed into the building and water floods the fire and before long the word comes out to us from inside that they've found the kid and he's dead. A pall falls over the firemen around me. Maybe it's just the effect of the smoke and the lack of sleep, but when the men who've found the kid come out to report to the chief, it seems to me I see tears in their eyes.

Somebody appears at one of the windows and calls my name, and I go over to him. It's Dennis. "You want to come in here?" he says. I say I don't know. All the horror of the charred bodies in the photos of the streetcar-fire victims from my childhood is coming back to me now and I'm getting a little rocky on my feet. "Come on," says Dennis, "I'll give you a hand."

I let myself be pulled through the smashed window into the smoky apartment which stinks of death, and I don't think I am going to make it.

"You want to see him?" says Dennis.

I shake my head.

"That's O.K.," he says gently. "I don't guess there's much point. You can't really tell it's a kid anymore anyway."

"I think I'd like to get out of here now," I say.

"O.K.," he says. "The first-due companies are going to do the mopping up and the . . . removal of the body in the body bag. We might as well go back to the engine."

We slosh through puddles of water on the floor and over piles of terrible-smelling burnt bedding and out through the smashed window again. Then we are outside and sloshing through more puddles of the water that was thrown on the fire. Lying in the puddles outside is a lot more burnt bedding and stuff that the firemen threw out of the fire, and also lying in the puddles are an overturned tricycle and a hollow rubber toy that squeaks underfoot as we pass. And as we walk I am being told something that I could cheerfully have lived the rest of my life without knowing—that burnt bodies become so brittle they break apart when you pick them up.

"Getting a D.O.A. is bad enough when it's an adult," says Dennis moodily. "You can always tell yourself, well, maybe he was drunk and smoking in bed or something and it was the guy's own fault. But when you get one and it's just a little kid . . ." He shakes his head. "By the way, we don't call them . . . what you may have heard anymore," he says.

"Roasts?"

"Yeah. Now we call them D.O.A.s."

We get back on the engine and it backs out of the street

and by now it's as light out as it's going to get and you can see how truly hideous a slum the South Bronx really is. The sky is filthy gray, and it has started to drizzle. It's the end of a very long, strange night and the beginning of a very ugly day. I ask Dennis if this has been a busier-than-usual night tour for him and he pauses to consider. "I'd say it was about average," he replies.

Iт's ten-thirty a.m. by the time I get home. My wife is in the kitchen, making toast in the toaster-oven. As I stand at the counter, trying to re-create for her the events of the past fifteen hours, I hear her give a little cry of terror and I look up to see that the toaster-oven has somehow caught fire.

Once I would have panicked—gone on a frenzied search for a fire extinguisher or a pot to fill with water. Now, at least temporarily deadened to the sight of flames, I hear myself sigh and watch myself walk up to the toaster-oven and blow out the fire with a single breath, as a child blows out a cake full of birthday candles.

A FEW months ago I was having dinner with my *Playboy* editor in a Chinese restaurant in Chicago, and midway between my Beef-and-Snow-Peas-Thousand-Fragrance and my Hot-and-Sour-Sherbet, he matter-of-factly slipped me the information that the guys at the mag had come up with what they thought was a rather amusing assignment for me: Basically, how would I feel about going to a sex orgy and writing about what it felt like?

"What do you mean," I said, "just go and observe and sort of take notes or what?"

"Well, we were thinking really more along the lines of your actually taking *part* in one," he said.

My chopsticks suddenly became too heavy to hold, and I lowered them carefully to the table. I should tell you at this point that I am so shy with women it took me till age twenty-three to lose my virginity, till age thirty to get married, and that as this is written at age thirty-six,* I am still unable to go to an ordinary cocktail party and chitchat with

* This was written in 1972.

folks like any regular grown-up person. The idea of sending old Greenburg to take part in an orgy was, frankly, tantamount to sending someone with advanced vertigo to do a tap dance on the wing of an airborne 747.

True, I had recently done an article on New York firefighters and in my research managed to overcome a deep phobia of fire by spending five months riding on fire trucks and racing into burning buildings with firemen—yet somehow that seemed tame by comparison with what I was now being asked to do. After all, the worst that could have happened to me in a burning building was that a flaming ceiling might have collapsed on me and crushed me to death. At an orgy there was the distinct possibility that I might be seriously laughed at in chorus.

"How about if I just go to an orgy and take notes?" I said.

My editor shrugged.

"Don't you think that'd be sort of a cop-out, journalistically?" he said.

"I suppose you're right," I said. "Look, give me a few days to think it over."

"PLAYBOY MAGAZINE wants you to do *what?*" said my wife.*

"Go to an orgy and kind of take part," I said.

"How about if you just go and take notes?" she said.

"Don't you think that'd be sort of a cop-out, journalistically?" I said.

"No," she said, "I don't."

"Oh," I said.

SEVERAL DAYS later, having mulled over all facets of the situation, having pondered the feats of Sir Edmund Hillary, Sir Francis Chichester, Ernie Pyle, Robert

* We speak here of a former wife.

Capa, Thor Heyerdahl, and others, having decided that, my experiences with firefighters notwithstanding, I had led a comparatively bland life and that only through the continual meeting of challenges and overcoming of fears was I going to attain any growth as a writer, and mainly, having learned from my agent the exact sum that *Playboy* was willing to pay me for this particular adventure, I was at length able to dispel most of my own doubts and a few of my wife's and I called my editor at *Playboy* and accepted the assignment.

THE FIRST person I contacted was an unattractive middle-aged lady in New York who is legendary for throwing the biggest orgies in town. I introduced myself to her on the phone, gave the name of a good mutual friend as a reference, and asked if I might see her to discuss in a sort of general way the broad spectrum of the group sex experience.

"I don't know why so many people call me and ask me about this subject," she said. "Just because I once gave an interview to some magazine in which I expressed a few opinions on group sex, suddenly I'm supposed to be some kind of expert on orgies. I really don't understand it. You probably thought I could get you invited to an orgy, didn't you?"

"Well . . . "

"Well, I can't. I don't have any contacts in that area at all, and I never did. Besides, I don't know a thing about you."

I offered to send her a copy of my recent book, *Scoring: A Sexual Memoir*. I said that reading it would tell her more about me than she might even wish to know. She said I was certainly welcome to send her the book, but she still didn't have any contacts in the group-sex circuit and didn't see how she could possibly be of any help to me. Then, just as she'd almost persuaded me that the several hundred stories

I'd heard about her were complete fabrication, she said rather offhandedly, "Tell me, is there a photo of you on the dust jacket, dear?"

THE LADY did not finally grant me an interview, but I was just about to leave for Los Angeles anyway, where, I was assured, the orgy thing was definitely more in the open. A *Playboy* contributing editor on the Coast, who had himself written a thing about swingers, promised to provide me on my arrival not only with several bona fide orgy contacts but also with a young lady who would willingly accompany me to whatever far-out type of thing I could get invited to.

"A thing you might start off with when you get here is one of the group-grope places that they have a lot of in L.A. They're supposed to raise your consciousness, heighten your sensitivity toward your fellow human beings, put you in touch with your feelings and stuff, but they're really mostly an excuse for a lot of people to get together and take off their clothes and screw."

I said that sort of deviousness had a certain comforting appeal. I flew to Los Angeles.

IT IS three minutes after I have checked into the Beverly Hills Hotel. I have given the bellhop what I consider to be a fairly generous tip, he stares at it as though I have just deposited several rabbit turds in his palm and stalks out of the room. I am now on the phone with the contributing editor, thirsting for names of group-grope places, bona fide orgy contacts, and the identity of the wanton woman who has volunteered to be my consort.

The contributing editor gives me the name of the wanton woman, and I burst out laughing because it is a dear platonic friend of mine from years back whose name is Linda Leeman, who is also a writer and who is about as wanton a woman as, say, the Queen Mother.

I ask for the names of the group-grope places. Actually, says my contributing editor, now that he thinks about it, the group-grope places are not such a good idea for me after all. Another writer is, even as we speak, putting the finishing touches on a piece for *Playboy* about changing lifestyles, and group-grope places turn out to figure quite prominently in his article. I am better off simply going to a normal no-nonsense orgy, he says.

I try to hide my disappointment at missing out on the less-threatening group-grope places and ask him for my normal no-nonsense orgy contacts. This too proves to be something of a disappointment.

"The main guy I wanted to put you in touch with is a guy named Mandell, who is in fact writing a book about orgies. But it turns out that Mandell is somewhat miffed that we've asked you and not him to do this article. He sort of considers L.A. orgies his turf. The other thing is, he claims his contacts aren't that fresh anymore. He used to be very into the orgy thing, but not anymore. He says he's settled down to a fairly meaningful relationship with two chicks he really digs. I do have one other contact for you, though. A guy named Artie throws orgies at his place every Saturday night. Call him up and tell him you're a close friend of Mandell's."

I call Artie and tell him what a great friend I am of Mandell's and ask him whether it's O.K. to attend his orgy this Saturday. Artie is polite but evasive. He says he may be having an orgy this Saturday and then again he may not. "It all depends on where my head is at," he says.

"Where do you *think* your head may be at?" I say. "I mean the thing is, I hate to be crass about it, but I do want to get to an orgy Saturday, and if *you're* not having one I'd like to find someone who is."

Artie says to call him about five on Saturday, by which time he will definitely know where his head is at.

It is Saturday about five and it doesn't matter where Artie's head is at, because my friend Linda has done some checking around and heard that Artie's parties are fairly well known among media people, and although she is neither willing to partake of the sexual activities nor even to take off her clothes, she fears meeting somebody she knows there. Instead she has come up with what she considers a much better orgy. This one is deep in the San Fernando Valley and is not apt to contain any people she knows. She already has the driving directions and the password and the information that the address we seek is a private home with Christmas tree lights strung outside. Since it is now the beginning of July I figure it should be fairly easy to spot. I tell Linda I will pick her up in about two hours. She seems very nervous. Her nervousness somewhat allays my own. Then I learn that her nervousness stems mainly from such decisions as what to wear, and I realize that our respective nervousnesses are not even in the same ball park.

I take a leisurely shower, then spend time applying after-shave cologne to places it has never before occurred to me to apply it. I grow perceptively more nervous. I grow so nervous that I begin to have contempt for *Linda's* nervousness. After all, what does *she* have to be nervous about? She's already decided she will neither have sex nor take off her clothes. I, on the other hand, am more or less philosophically committed to both.

What if my body, slim and trendy by New York standards, is thought to be skinny and slug-white by well-muscled, sun-bronzed Angelenos? What if my dork, regulation-sized by New York locker-room standards, is dwarfed by acrobatic hyperactive valley orgiasts? What if I'm unable to keep it up or even *get* it up into a polite state of erection? What if, the thought now strikes me as my nervousness creeps over the line into panic and nausea, what if I get really sick and puke my guts out all over everybody at the orgy? What if, God forbid, I contract a venereal disease—not even the Syph or the Clap but a new kind* we've learned about from terrific Dr. David Reuben that you don't even know you *have* until about twelve years later when suddenly your brain turns to zabaglione and your dork into an ocarina, and the virus that causes it not only doesn't respond to antibiotics but *thrives* on them?

I take a flask of vodka out of my suitcase and gulp down half of it. It has no apparent effect. I go into the bathroom and take another shower. Why am I taking a second shower? To wash off future dirt?

I must snap out of this. I must pull myself together. I must do this for the sake of the editors at *Playboy*—the sadistic, seriously deranged editors at *Playboy*—who are counting on me and on my professionalism to complete this assignment.

I polish off the rest of the vodka in the flask. I snap out of it. I pull myself together. I lurch out of my hotel room and into the lobby, nearly colliding with a succession of guests, and manage to make it all the way to my rented car without actually falling onto the ground.

SATURDAY, nine p.m. We have parked the car hard by the house with the July Christmas tree lights and we ring the bell. From inside the house comes the tinkle of music and merry, possibly unclothed voices. A stocky clothed gentleman comes to the door and asks if he can help us.

---

* This was written before herpes and AIDS were invented.

Linda has forgotten the password, forgotten who sent us, forgotten everything, and begins babbling hysterically. I withdraw into a state of quasi catatonia. Well, what is the gentleman at the door going to do, after all, call the cops? ("Hello, police? There's a couple of writers here trying to crash our orgy . . .")

At length the man at the door wearies of Linda's babbling, mumbles that the usual practice is to pre-screen guests, but that in our case he'll merely take our $7 admission fee and let us in.

I hand him a crumpled ball of sweaty dollar bills. He reaches for a card and asks our names.

"Uh . . . Linda Lyman," replies Linda Leeman in a strange high voice.

"Dan Greenburg," I gasp, not having the strength to even make it as far as Greenstein.

The man laboriously prints out our names, then turns to me.

"It's a soft swing," he says pointedly.

"Uh, what?" I say.

"It's a soft swing. If a chick says no, don't push it."

"Oh, all right," I say, hoping to give the impression that I'm more used to *hard* swings where, presumably, if a chick says no you throw her up against the wall, slap the hell out of her and rape her.

We enter the orgy. We look around.

If we did not absolutely beyond any doubt know that it was an orgy, we might very well have mistaken it for a high school bring-your-own-bottle party. Most people present have, in fact, brought their own bottles. They have also brought things in homey covered-casserole dishes. The lighting is soft and multicolored. Dance music comes from a radio. Everyone in sight is fully clothed.

Directly ahead of us is a sort of combination kitchen-ballroom. That is, it contains a sink, stove, refrigerator, and tiny dance floor. About three couples are dancing. The rest are talking in twos or standing around looking pitiful.

The age range is early thirties to mid-fifties. The men mainly wear short-sleeved flowered shirts and slightly-too-short slacks, the women a wide variety of things from pants suits to hot pants to long dresses. There is one woman who is well over six feet tall. There is another who may weigh as much as three hundred pounds. There is a moderately attractive Eurasian lady with a high-necked shiny silk dress slit all the way up her thigh who looks like she spends her non-orgy time seating people in Chinese restaurants. There are many men with long sideburns and skinny mustaches. They are not, how shall one put it, the sort of folks one would have voluntarily selected as sex partners. On the other hand, one had not been consulted.

There is a great profusion of signs in day-glo lettering posted all about, exhorting one to smile, to have a happy day, to be friendly, to do one's own thing. There is one particularly prominent sign that catches my eye and that I am told is the Swinger's Credo:

> I do my thing and you do your thing.
> I am not in this world to live up to your
>   expectations,
> And you are not in this world to live up to mine.
> You are you and I am I,
> And if by chance we find each other
> It's beautiful.
>
> —Frederick S. Perls

Questions of whether I am I or I am me aside, it seems a reasonable enough credo. Linda and I stand there, reading the credo for perhaps the fortieth time, terrified of doing anything else, when I spot a person who looks like someone I might be able to talk to without passing out. He is a young person wearing blue jeans, as I am, and wearing rather long hair tied back in a ponytail, which I am not, but the point is that he looks about as out of place as I feel.

Linda and I introduce ourselves to him and discover that his name is Jesse, that he is from Oklahoma, and that he is a guitarist. I see this as hopeful—a Person in the Arts. Actually, says Jesse, to fill in the gaps, moneywise, between guitar gigs, he sells tires. How long has it been between guitar gigs, I ask. About eight years, Jesse figures.

We ask Jesse to show us around and he does. He points out a room adjacent to the kitchen-ballroom that contains a movie projector and screen and several cans of stag film and that also contains several clothed couples sitting around getting acquainted. He points out a large empty bedroom with a large empty bed and indicates that there are three more bedrooms, a shower, and a sauna right up those stairs there.

"Say," he says, "how'd you like to see the Caves?"

We say sure, wondering whether we are in for stalactite-stalagmite distinction things and whether in fact this entire setup is really an orgy or merely a giant seven-dollar put-on.

Jesse leads us through a beaded curtain into an area that looks like a fourth-rate Jean Cocteau fantasy of a Pullman sleeping car. It is a room that has been divided up into cubicles on two levels, the floors of which are mattresses covered by sheets, the walls of which are flush with the dimensions of the mattresses, and the ceilings of which are scarcely high enough to sit up without bumping your head against them. The whole thing has been covered with charcoal-grey foam rubber spattered with day-glo paint and lit with black light. The effect of the black light is that white things like teeth and sheets appear florescent purple and vaguely stained. Whatever else one may want at an orgy, it cannot possibly be lighting that reveals teeth and sheets as fluorescent purple and vaguely stained. And vague stains there assuredly are. On every tooth and sheet in the place.

Jesse excuses himself, saying he must get back to his little woman and introduce her around. He steps over us as we huddle in the crawl space between cubicles, and just as we are deciding what to do next, a clothed couple comes straight through the beaded curtain, ducks into a cubicle to our right, and immediately articles of clothing come flying out into the crawl space. I turn to gape, and although my view of the couple is limited to toes at one end and lower thighs at the other, I can see by the position and the motion of the legs that definite intercourse without foreplay has just commenced.

Scarcely has the first couple begun than a second couple enters and steps into the cubicle to our immediate left. Clothes once more come flying out, and although my view of this couple is only from shoulders to waists, it is apparent that these folks also have little truck with foreplay.

A third couple enters the sanctuary (has someone outside blown a whistle?) and climbs nimbly over our backs and up a ladder into a cubicle directly above our heads. More articles of clothing come flying out—we are covered with it like floppy flakes of freshly fallen snow—and soon we are surrounded on three sides by copulating (and, one might add, mysteriously lubricated) couples.

Since Linda and I are loath to make the commitment of crawling out of the crawl space into an actual cubicle ourselves and since we are clearly about to become a major traffic jam, we back out of the Caves and return to the staging areas.

The rest of the house is much as we left it. Couples still dance in the kitchen and sit chatting in the porno-movie room. Most of them are still clothed. One clean-cut young lad in Jockey shorts enters somewhat breathlessly and is razzed about copulatory fatigue. A poignant-looking middle-aged lady in toreadors tries unsuccessfully to pick him up, then turns to me and asks me something about ice cubes which sounds faintly suggestive. The lad in the Jockey shorts jogs off and is replaced by a definitely naked, seriously pudgy fellow.

Linda is standing three yards away from me with her back turned, as the naked pudgy fellow approaches her from behind and puts his hands on her waist. Linda, thinking it is me, grasps the hands, turns around, sees the pudginess and the nakedness, and bolts for the bathroom. The naked pudgy fellow shrugs and pads away.

Up the stairs one can see a great deal of frenzied activity. Several naked persons of both sexes, most with dumpy bodies, are running back and forth between bedrooms, showers and sauna, giggling immoderately. A clothed person at my elbow notes my absorption with the upstairs activity and suggests I take a shower. I say thanks but I've already had two so far this evening. Then I spot Linda darting out of the downstairs bathroom, still somewhat shaken.

As we stand there, trying to decide whether leaving is a permissible cop-out, a stocky man with a short-sleeved shirt and a pencil-thin moustache approaches, introduces himself as Freddy, informs us he is a stunt man at M-G-M, and indicates in no uncertain terms his immediate fondness for Linda. The way he indicates this fondness is by placing his hand behind her neck and drawing her toward him by her hair. I recall the admonition that this is a soft swing and wonder whether Freddy has heard. He has. Freddy has been a member of this particular club for years. He and his wife are members of *five* swingers' clubs, he says, but this club is definitely the best.

"What makes this one the best?" asks Linda, deftly disentangling her hair from his hand.

"The *people*," says Freddy, "the *people*."

Our minds boggle as we try to summon up images of the caliber of people at the other four clubs.

Freddy asks whether we have seen the pool. We have not. Leading Linda now by the hand rather than by the hair, he escorts us into the backyard and a floodlit swimming pool that is both unoccupied and unheated.

"This is the pool," says Freddy, perhaps fearing that we believe it to be something more sinister.

I stick my hand into the water and remark how cold it is, whereupon we are treated to our first bona fide tacky sex joke of the evening:

"No sense ruining a perfectly good member in that cold water," Freddy says.

We chuckle politely, but apparently Freddy fears that the double-entendre has somehow eluded us.

"No sense ruining a perfectly good member in that cold water," Freddy says once more.

Fearing yet another repetition of the joke, we swiftly change the subject. We ask Freddy how he came to be a swinger.

"Well sir," he says, "I guess you could say I became a swinger in order to save my marriage."

"How's that?" I say.

"Before we became swingers," he says, "hell, I was screwing every single one of my wife's girlfriends."

"And now?"

Freddy's face breaks into a beatific smile.

"Since the day we became swingers," he says proudly, "I have been completely faithful."

"Tell me, Freddy," I say, "how do you feel when you know that your wife has just had sex with another man?"

"Just great," he says. "Matter of fact, I'm never so turned on to her as when she's just got done making it with another guy."

"So do you sometimes just make love to her right then and there?"

"Oh no," says Freddy, as if explaining to a very small child that we do *not* make ca-ca in our pants.

"Why not?" I say.

"Well, sir, we tend to frown on that sort of thing around here," he says. "Oh, I don't mean that it never *happens* that a man has sex with his own wife at one of these parties, it's just that we tend to frown on it. Why, I remember one time a guy and his wife started upstairs to one of the bedrooms . . ." He chuckles at the memory. "We booed them all the way up the stairs."

It now occurs to me that although I have thus far this evening heard the phrases "We don't put that down" and "Do your own thing" a number of times, I have also heard the phrase "We tend to frown on that" quite a little too. I ask Freddy what other types of things they tend to frown on at these shindigs.

"Well, we tend to frown on things like . . . oh, like more than two people making it with each other at the same time . . . or people watching other people while they're making it. . . . We tend to frown on people who come here without partners. . . . We frown on homosexuality. . . . And we frown on somebody seeing somebody on the outside that they've met at one of our parties."

"Why is that?" I say, but I think I already know.

"Because," says Freddy. "That's adultery."

THE ORGY in the valley has not been devoid of value, but neither has it provided me with the opportunity I so ambivalently seek: to take part in the festivities and take note of my reactions.

"There's a place I've heard of that we probably ought to check out," says Linda. "It's called Topley Too."

"Where is it?" I say.

"I don't know exactly, but they run ads in the *Free Press*."

Celebrate the 4th
with a

BANG!

In fact
spend the holiday at
our place and you'll
probably get

BANGED A LOT!

Special events Jul. 1–4
And then we have

Mon.
Tues.   } GET NAKED NIGHT

As if that's not enuf

WED. NITE
STRIP CONTEST

Cash prizes * Bare asses

THURS. COUPLES NITE

Would you like to have
a strip contest at our
Thurs. nite couples party?
*   Dancing nightly   *
No door chg. – No cover

*   *   *

TOPLEY TOO

8875 Pico   *   271-4370

*   *   *

BANKAMERICARD & MASTER OK

—Ad in the L.A. *Free Press*,
June 30, 1972

I decide to skip Topley Too.

Notwithstanding my contributing editor's admonitions to steer clear of what he termed the group-grope places, I feel that this type of place may be the least traumatic way for me to get my feet (or whatever) wet. I recall that a well-known writer I am friendly with in New York has mentioned visiting one of these places, and I put in a long-distance call to him.

My writer friend has indeed spent time at the best one of these places, but seems somewhat disturbed to learn of my interest. He is writing something about this topic himself and feels a certain proprietary interest in the place.* I assure him I have no intention of trying to scoop him and that if I do write about the place I won't even identify it by name. He says he couldn't in all conscience ask another writer not to write about something because he happened to be covering it too, but I sense his extreme discomfort and I don't push it. I don't even ask him a name of a person to call there.

It has begun to seem to me that so many writers are now writing articles and books about orgy-related topics that it's like the Communist movement of the 1940s and 1950s, where half the people at every cell meeting were F.B.I. men. I would not be much surprised to find that half the people present at any given orgy in Los Angeles or New York are writers doing research, all interviewing and/or fucking each other, professionally if not carnally.

I telephone the place my writer friend has spent time at, and I am referred to their public relations man. Unwilling for the moment to dwell on either the sociological ramifications or the punning possibilities of their having a public relations man, I tell him quite straightforwardly of my in-

---

* Too many years have passed for this to remain a blind item. The writer was Gay Talese, what he was writing was *Thy Neighbor's Wife*, and the place in question was Sandstone.

terest in visiting. He agrees to the visit and gives detailed directions.

AFTER nearly an hour's drive along the ocean and then up narrow, winding roads into the mountains, Linda and I arrive at our destination. It's five-thirty p.m. and the views in all directions from our mountaintop are spectacular. We discover we are both every bit as nervous now as we were at the orgy in the valley, so we each take long pulls on my flask of vodka.

The grounds seem deserted. We approach the nearest building and enter. What we have entered is the immense living room of the main house. A dozen attractive young people sit reading, playing cards or chess, or chatting quietly. They are all quite nude.

We chat and I learn that the place is a sort of nudist colony, for want of a better term, that has ten full-time adult residents and about two hundred or so members who come there to swim, sunbathe, and mainly, make love to any of the other members who happen to be in the mood. The feeling is that members should be free to have one primary intimate love-sex relationship and a number of secondary ones, that the secondary ones won't detract from the primary one but will make it even better.

Before we know it we've been talking an hour and a half. They ask if we'd like to go for a swim. (It is clear one does not swim in swimsuits here.) Linda is hesitant. I say sure. They get us towels and point the way to the indoor swimming pool.

THE pool is deserted. First I, and then Linda, take off our clothes and our glasses and enter the warm bath-tubby water. We are not splashing around for more than ten minutes when we perceive that a small blurred group of people has come into the pool building and shucked off its clothes and entered the water. Tragically, both Linda and I are so nearsighted without our glasses it's impossible to even see what they look like. There is a certain amount of splashing around and there are voices, and then the voices become still and it strikes me that what we may have a scant few yards away from us are two or so couples engaged in some level of foreplay. For all I know they may even be screwing.

"Listen," I whisper to Linda, "I don't want to be so obvious as to actually paddle over and ask what they're doing, but what do *you* think is going on over there to our right?"

Linda squints unobtrusively in the proper direction.

"It's either a guy hugging and kissing a lady or hugging and kissing a beach ball," she confides.

AFTER a pleasant swim, a pleasant dinner and no *visible* orgying, we prepare to go. We learn that the main reason we haven't seen any lovemaking (assuming that what we vaguely saw in the pool wasn't lovemaking) is that their major get-togethers happen to take place on Wednesday and Saturday nights and today is Tuesday.

IT IS two weeks later. I have spent a fruitless forty or fifty phone calls trying to drum up an orgy to go to in New York and I am running out of contacts, patience, and time. Several staff members of *Playboy* call to find out how I'm doing and to ask when they can expect the manuscript. I tell them I can't even *begin* writing the manuscript till I've taken part in an orgy and I catalog the difficulties I've had in the last two weeks. There is no denying the pressure. I have less than a week now to either come up with a viable orgy or else miss my deadline and be forced to beg out of my assignment altogether.

And then—success. A friend of a friend of a friend has found a chap who used to be very into the orgy thing, and although he has mostly dropped out of it now (he has a meaningful relationship with *three* chicks he really digs), he has agreed to throw an orgy in my honor. It is to take place this coming Wednesday in his posh East Side apartment and it will begin promptly at nine p.m. Sensing my nervousness (no mean trick, this), the host kindly suggests I stop by his place about four-thirty Wednesday afternoon to meet him and look over the apartment, thereby eliminating two of the many unknown factors I'll be forced to deal with when my hour of trial arrives.

WEDNESDAY, four-thirty. My host is a tall, athletic-looking guy in his thirties—intelligent, articulate, and nice. His name is Walt. It is not clear what Walt does for a living, although one has heard he is a gambler and has managed to gamble away a Chris-Craft, a Maserati, and a much more sumptuous apartment than the not *un*sumptuous one we are standing in. He shows me around. Good modern furniture. Chrome and leather. Fur rugs. Large wall mirrors in the bedroom. "In my last apartment," says Walt wistfully, "the mirrors were on the ceiling."

"What do you do, Walt?" I say.

"What I do, Dan, is make love. That's mainly what I do. It's what I *like* best, it's what I *do* best, and everything else is just to fill in the gaps."

Walt estimates he has made love to about a thousand women in his fifteen years of orgygoing.

A dog of spaniel descent enters and gives me the once-over.

"That dog," says Walt, "just happens to give the best head in town. He's not pushy about it though. He won't come over and do anything unless you invite him."

Walt fixes me a scotch and water, as an attractive young woman of foreign descent finishes tidying up and as delivery boys arrive with cases of liquor and mix. Another young woman—the caterer, says Walt—has just left after laying in a supply of delicacies like Devil Dogs, Good Humor bars, and Reddi Wip. Walt himself has already spent a lot of time in preparation.

"A good orgy has to be as carefully choreographed as a good ballet," he says. "I've already chosen the cast, set the lighting, planned the flow of the evening. I preprogrammed all the music you'll be hearing tonight on the tape deck. I polished up the vibrators and the dildoes, and I told the maid to put out the dark sheets."

My host is obviously getting a great kick out of his role, and when I leave, I feel I could not be in better hands. He says he'll see me at nine p.m. sharp.

MY DATE for the evening is an attractive young actress named Mary-Jenifer Mitchell who has been in *Oh! Calcutta!* and *The Dirtiest Show in Town* and who is on loan from her preposterously generous boyfriend. (When you call them and they aren't home, their answering machine says, "Please leave your name, phone number, and favorite erogenous zones.") Mary makes no pronouncements about nonparticipation in this evening's festivities, she merely requests that I use her real name in my article.

"Have you been to lots of orgies, Mary?"

She thinks a bit.

"I don't guess I've really *been* to any," she says. "But of course I've *thrown* a couple."

Mary, like Walt, is somehow able to sense my nervousness and suggests I meet her an hour before the orgy for a drink. What makes anybody think I'm nervous?

WEDNESDAY, nine p.m. I have showered, shaved, cologned, and anointed my body with precious oils, staving off repeated attacks of nausea and the shakes with the better part of a bottle of Meyer's Rum. I have met Mary at a bar and together we have consumed more liquor and

I have gotten us a cab for the remaining three blocks to the orgy due to serious doubts I will be able to keep putting one leg in front of the other for that vast a distance. We are leaning against our host's doorjamb and ringing his bell. He opens the door and ushers us into the apartment, which has been magically transformed into a pleasure garden.

There are candles. There is incense. There is exotic music. There are my host's three attractive girls, clothed. There is my host himself, clothed. I am to put myself completely in his hands. He will guide me through this entire experience. He will tell me exactly what I ought to do at every step.

"I think you ought to sit down," he says.

I do. Mary sits down next to me. There is a definite lack of spontaneous conversation among those present. There is a ring of the doorbell. There is another couple. There is passed around for sniffing certain powders, certain poppers. There is yet another ring of the doorbell. There is our final couple.

"I think we need your chairs now," says my host to me and to Mary. "Why don't you two go into the bedroom."

We certainly can't fight logic like that. We get up. We go into the candle-lit bedroom. This is it. This is really it. There is absolutely no way to chicken out now. We have passed the point of no return. I smile at Mary. She smiles at me. We take off our clothes. I take off my glasses. I can't see a thing. We get into bed. We get to work.

A personage has materialized at our side, divested himself of his clothing and joined us in the bed. It is our host. He begins kissing and licking Mary's unclaimed areas. I wonder how I feel about having another guy make love to my date and decide the thought is not appropriate to the situation. My host disappears. Then he reappears, this time with one of his girls. There are four of us in bed. Then six. *Six naked people in a huge bed somewhere on Manhattan's posh East Side, all having some form of sex together and I, by God, am one of them.*

I keep thinking to myself: "Look how I'm really doing this. Look how I'm at least physically a part of all this. Look how I'm at least intermittently potent. Look how God is not hurling bolts of lightning to incinerate me." And I keep thinking how detached and on-the-outside-looking-in I feel and it's like being at a screening of a very blurred stag film and I keep wanting to yell "Focus!" to the projectionist.

At one point in all this activity I hear my host say "O.K., Greenburg, time to fuck a stranger," and I feel myself being lifted up off one lady and onto another. Good old Walt. Keeping things moving. Choreographing. Bless him. I adjust myself to the new lady, nod a shy hello and set to work.

At another point in the evening, I find myself fondling and kissing an arm I believe belongs to the young woman I am currently entertaining, then discover that the arm belongs to my host. I mumble apologies but see they're not needed. My host's concentration is elsewhere than his arm. He and another lady are, by coincidence, busily at work on the same lady I'm at work on, he kissing the lady's mouth, she kissing the lady's left breast. I apologize for apologizing and return to the task at hand.

It is two a.m. We all stop and go into the living room for snacks and such. I learn that one of the men present is an investment broker, one is an attorney. One of the women is a graduate student in English Lit, another of the women some sort of fashion designer, a third it seems to me is a manicurist. I could be wrong about this. I could be wrong about a lot of things. Like whether or not I'm really here.

By three-thirty it is over. We put on our clothes, thank our host, and stand at the door exchanging polite nice-to-meet-you's. I want to ask "Was it good for all of you too?" but I don't. I say to the possible manicurist that I'm not sure whether I've had her but, if so, it was nice. She laughs, thinking I'm kidding.

I put Mary in a cab and walk slowly home, feeling very odd

indeed. I have managed to fulfill my mission by severing both the peaks and valleys from my emotional electrocardiogram, and the result is that I cannot be completely sure of what has happened. I feel very detached. Surreal. Sophisticated. Blasé. *Fatigué*. European. Old. How do you like that—me, a fella that's been to orgies.

My wife awakes as I get into bed.

"How was it?" she asks.

"I don't know," I say. "I'm trying to figure it out."

IT TAKES me a full day to get over the hangover, a full three days to get over the sense of surreality. I call my *Playboy* editor in Chicago with the news that I've finally finished my research, had my orgy, and am going to be able to make my deadline after all.

"How did it go at the orgy?" he says. "Any trouble?"

"Oh no, not really," I say.

"There wasn't any trouble?"

"Not really."

"You mean you didn't even throw up?"

"Not really," I say. "I did feel a little nauseous beforehand, but that went away by the time we actually started. Everything worked out fine."

There's a brief silence at the other end of the line.

"You sonofabitch," says my editor, and now, suddenly, I realize just how much of a set-up this whole assignment has been: Let's send old Greenburg into a situation where he can't fail to make an ass of himself, and what a fine giggle we'll all have afterward at his expense.

"I'm sorry things didn't go worse," I say, "I really am."

I FINISH the first draft of this article and that night my wife and I are at a cocktail party and I am trying very hard not to act too overpoweringly blasé/fatigué/European/old. A rather straight married lady we know announces she has just had her first experience skinnydipping. Before I even have time to appreciate the irony, I have completely forgotten how blasé/*fatigué*/European/old I am, I have forgotten all about the six naked bodies on the bed in the posh East Side apartment, and I am pumping the straight married lady for every last detail of her skinnydipping experience like some horny high school sophomore.

THIS is about black magic. It is also about how, without intending to, folks like me get caught up in things that become more and more entangling till one day they find they are into it up to their eyeballs and it is no longer easy to become unentangled.

The time is September 1974 and I am in a tiny town in the Highlands of Scotland called Drumnadrochit. Drumnadrochit is on the shore of Loch Ness, and how I happen to be there is that I am hanging out with a team of Japanese who claim to be hunting the Loch Ness Monster but who seem far more interested in holding press conferences than in hunting monsters.

It is at one of these press conferences that I meet a long-haired, bearded, twenty-year-old, American student named Lee Frank. Lee has spent the summer tending underwater cameras and sonar equipment in Loch Ness for an outfit called the Academy of Applied Science, who seem somewhat more serious about monster hunting than the Japanese. Lee and I hit it off right away, and he remarks to me in a kind of offhand way that from what he's seen up here in the past few months

Loch Ness is a very weird place and there are far more sinister things going on than the Loch Ness Monster.

Like what? I say. Oh, various occult things, he says. Like what? I say. Oh, like corpse lights, he says. Uh, what are corpse lights? I say. Well, he says, when people die up here a luminous shape is often seen leaving the body at the moment of death, which then proceeds directly to the site of burial. Mmmm. What else besides corpse lights? I say. Well, says Lee, he has heard that a ghost ship is seen on the Loch itself every twenty years. And he knows of a house in this area where the ghost of a small blonde girl appears and pleads for help to any female guest who happens to be sleeping in the kid's former bedroom. And he knows of another house in the area where the ghost of a well-dressed gentleman appears in *his* former bedroom, where he committed suicide a few years ago. The very hotel I am staying in, says Lee, is said to have a ghost which is frequently heard walking right up the walls.

A local family Lee knows is visited periodically by a mysterious black soccer-sized ball that bounds merrily into the living room, bounces around on the floor and on the mantelpiece, then disappears. The ball has never been rude or nasty, so the family has gotten rather casual about its appearances. One night a guest was with them when the ball bounded in and went into its shtick. The guest regarded the ball thoughtfully for a moment, then said, "Ah, I see you have one of those too."

As a matter of fact, says Lee, the neighborhood is so glutted with corpse lights, phantom soccer balls, and ghosts of one thing and another that in June of 1973 a writer named F. W. Holliday brought the Chief Exorcist of the Church of England (you probably didn't even know they *have* one of those) up here to exorcise the Loch of its evil influences. Immediately following the exorcism, Holliday took the exorcist, Reverend Ormand, to the home of a local couple named Cary for a little post-exorcism chitchat. As they sat bantering with Wing

Commander and Mrs. Cary, a swirling black cloud appeared just outside the Carys' living-room window, kicking up the rosebushes. Three explosions rocked the house and a beam of intense white light went from the swirling black cloud to the forehead of F. W. Holliday and then vanished.

Reverend Ormand allowed as how the exorcism hadn't probably been so successful after all and said that they were in grave danger. He warned them not to leave the house till morning and suggested a kind of first-aid ritual to get them through the night which involved slapping a crucifix on your forehead and sticking your thumb in a glass of water. Commander Cary wasn't buying crucifixes on foreheads and thumbs in glasses of water, but they tricked him into it, I am told, while he was bending over the stove. The next day Ormand and Holliday hightailed it out of the Highlands, never to return. The swirling black cloud, says Lee, is known as a black bogle and is not an uncommon phenomenon hereabouts.

Lee asks if I have ever heard of Aleister Crowley. I have, sort of. Crowley was a big black magician some years back who referred to himself as The Beast. Lee says that Crowley owned a house on Loch Ness called Boleskine, which is now owned by Led Zeppelin. Lee has heard rumors that a black magician is currently living there and figures it might be a good place to begin our investigation of the occult. We could take a ride up to Boleskine tomorrow, he says, assuming I'm not afraid. I say tomorrow is fine, and I'm not afraid. Well, not that much, anyway.

Conjuring up Abra-Melin demons is a ticklish business. Crowley successfully raised them—"the lodge and the terrace," he wrote, "soon became peopled with shadowy shapes"—but he was unable to control them. [They] entered the house [Boleskine] and wrought havoc: his coachman, hitherto a teetotaller, fell into *delerium tremens*; a clairvoyante whom he had brought from

London returned there and became a prostitute; his house-keeper, "unable to bear the eeriness of the place," vanished; a madness settled upon one of the workmen employed on the estate and he tried to kill the Laird of Boleskine. Even the butcher down in the village was affected through Crowley's casually jotting down on one of his bills the name of two demons . . . while cutting up a joint for a customer, the butcher accidentally severed his femoral artery and promptly died.

—from *The Great Beast*, by John Symonds

SINCE neither Lee nor I have a car at this point, we manage to con a British reporter named Sydney Burton into driving us around the far side of the Loch to Boleskine. Sydney Burton is a short, gray-haired chap with a jaunty manner and a perky military mustache. He is at Loch Ness covering the Japanese monster hunt for the Yorkshire *Post*. It is a big mistake to take Sydney to Boleskine, but we do not know this at the time.

The drive to Boleskine is quite picturesque. By and by, we pull up before a massive gate to a private road. On the gate is a sign which says ANIMALS DRIVE SLOWLY. Whether this is a warning to human motorists, an observation on how animals handle vehicles, or a caveat to nonhuman drivers is not entirely clear. Throwing reason to the winds, we open the gate and proceed up the steep road to a low one-story stuccolike house in poor repair. Over the entrance to the house I note that the skull of a goat has been nailed. Lee needlessly points out that this is the symbol of the Devil.

The house appears, at least from the outside, to be abandoned and devoid of life. I make this observation aloud, along with the suggestion that we might as well leave, when a bearded man and a large German shepherd materialize in back of us. Sydney and Lee take a speedy vote and elect me our spokesman.

I take a tentative half-step in the direction of man and dog and, smiling faintly, say I'm from *Esquire* magazine and these gentlemen and myself have heard a lot about Boleskine and we sure are sorry to be trespassing on private property and all but we sure hope we can look around a bit if it isn't going to be a horrible inconvenience. Man and dog nod seriously and neither one seems on the verge of biting me, so I relax a little. I add that I have always been fascinated by the life and work of Aleister Crowley (a flagrant untruth) and that I'd heard that the folks who now owned Boleskine know a lot about Crowley.

The bearded guy says that if we like we can go inside and talk to a chap named Eric, who knows considerably more about Crowley and various other Dark Things than *he* does. I say we'd be tickled to death to meet Eric, hoping I'm not being taken too literally. The bearded guy leads us past a couple of sheep and through the doorway with the goat's skull above it and on into the house.

The house itself is dark, cavernous, and very sparsely furnished. I do not immediately spot any Abra-Melin demons, but then I don't know what they look like. A thin young American with an angular face, sandy hair, torn blue jeans, and a soft Southern accent is introduced to us as Eric Hill, the person who Knows About Crowley. I repeat the little intro I'd cooked up outside and Eric says he'd be delighted to show us around and tell us whatever we want to know about Crowley.

Eric explains that the house is owned by Jimmy Page, the lead guitarist of the Led Zeppelin, who is not in Scotland at present, and that Eric and his wife and child are living there temporarily, as are the man we'd met outside and *his* wife and child. Eric leads us down a dark hallway into a room with a bare wood floor and no furniture, but which commands a marvelous view of the Loch. This room, Eric explains, used to be Crowley's temple. This is where Crowley practiced his magical rites.

As Eric starts to fill us in on Crowley in a pleasant, chatty manner, a small blond boy of about two, wearing shoes several sizes too large, tramps noisily into the room and begins methodically clomping over every inch of the floor. Eric takes no notice of him and neither does Lee or Sydney, so for a while I begin to wonder idly if the child is perhaps not a child but a demon. Tiring of merely clomping *around* us, the child-or-demon elects to clomp *upon* us, whereupon Eric notices him for the first time and, calling him Aleister, tells him to clomp around someplace else, for God's sake. I judge the kid to be Crowley's namesake rather than some incarnation of Crowley himself, and Eric goes on talking to us. The youthful Aleister takes no notice whatever of Eric's reproof.

Between clomps we learn that Aleister Crowley was not at all the nasty fellow portrayed in the press, that he was in fact neither bad nor good, but a delightfully amoral man who was a great intellectual, poet, mountaineer, practitioner of magic, and the originator of nothing less than a whole new philosophy of life, the cornerstone of which is "Do what thou wilt shall be the whole of the law."

Sydney Burton, who has so far been listening to Eric as politely as the rest of us, now decides to become a parody of Establishment Man as portrayed in youth cult movies. Who are the Led Zeppelin, asks Sydney, and haven't they become passé like the Beatles and why would they be interested in Crowley and in black magic and how could black magic be as innocuous as Eric described it and wasn't it in fact a dangerous and antisocial movement that ought to be stamped out?

Eric quite justifiably cools off toward us and politely explains, perhaps to ward off further attack, that he himself is a practitioner of magic, an avid student of Crowley if not a disciple, and that he is into everything that Crowley was, including magical rituals, poetry writing, and mountain climbing.

"Wasn't Crowley a homo?" says Sydney. Lee and I wince and begin edging Sydney toward the door. But Sydney is not ready to quit. Terrierlike, he sinks his journalistic teeth into Eric's pant leg and begins to tug at him with hostile and non-sequiturish questions: Why is the Led Zeppelin called by such a silly name and what does it mean and can Eric state Crowley's philosophy in three sentences and isn't Crowley's philosophy the same as that of Charles Manson?

Lee and I each take Sydney by one of his arms, lift him off the ground, and half carry him to the door. We apologize to Eric *sotto voce* and advise him we'll call him later that night and arrange a time to return, devoid of Sydney.

SYDNEY drops us off at Lee's shack and continues on to the hotel. Lee is supervising the Academy's underwater camera installation from a rustic hut he's built on a sheep meadow at the edge of the Loch. The meadow itself is owned by the aforementioned Wing Commander and Mrs. Cary of swirling-black-cloud fame. Lee drops in to see the Carys and makes the mistake of telling them we've been to Boleskine. Perhaps fearing further onslaughts of swirling black clouds, the Carys holler at Lee that he was crazy to go to Boleskine and they threaten to throw him and the Academy off their land if he has any notion of going back there.

Lee and I drop in on Nick Witchell, Lee's associate. Nick is an English law student who happens to be one of the Loch Ness Monster's leading biographers. Nick has a shack on the Carys' land not far from Lee's and is helping to maintain the Academy's vigil for the Monster. He is quite fascinated with our description of Boleskine and of the talk with Eric, but when we tell him we plan to go back there, he seems genuinely alarmed. He warns us both in his cultured English accent not to tamper with the forces of evil. I ask him if he seriously believes there are such things as forces of evil. He tents his fingers together and frowns.

"Why fool about with something you don't understand?" he says at last.

IT IS the following day. Despite the warnings of the Carys and of Nick Witchell, we have decided to fool about with something we don't understand. We rent a car and begin the hour-long drive around the Loch to Boleskine. The warnings have made us jumpy and the sensation of driving a right-hand-drive car on the left-hand side of the road has made me even jumpier. I keep drifting into the wrong lane following turns, and the blare of outraged horns keeps reminding me I'm in a strange country. It is almost a relief to get to the pink one-lane job on the far side of the Loch and to stop concentrating on keeping to the left. Lee and I joke nervously about what Eric may introduce us to at Boleskine, now that we are free of Sydney. Midnight rites with human sacrifices? Ritual orgies with demon nymphomaniacs? Suddenly, around a curve comes a huge tractor-trailer, hurtling toward us in the road's only lane. Thinking fast, I veer off the road and down into a deepish roadside ditch.

Lee and I crawl out of the car, which is now tilted downward at a crazy angle, and discover that we are unhurt. The tractor-trailer has stopped, and three burly Scots in dirty coveralls have without a word emerged from it and hunkered down under my rear axle and are trying to pull the car out of the ditch by hand. I smile embarrassedly and apologize for driving into the ditch, as if there was anything else I could have done. They nod seriously, attach chains to the rear axle and to their truck. They get back into the truck and inch it forward and haul my car back onto the road. I thank them profusely for their help. "Well now," says one of them in this very matter-of-fact Scottish burr, "we couldn't leave ye sittin' all day long in a ditch, now could we?"

We are under way again and Lee is telling me how he's heard that people often have road accidents on the way to Boleskine. It is more likely that this is due to the narrow one-lane road than to any forces of evil, but our accident has made us jumpier nonetheless.

We arrive at Boleskine nearly two hours late. We get out of the car and make our way past several morose sheep, the German shepherd, two geese, and a rather worried-looking goat, and enter the house. "Close the door," yells Eric's wife Iris, "or the sheep will come in and shit on the floor!"

Eric leads us into a small high-ceilinged bedroom adjoining Crowley's temple, and after accepting our apologies about Sydney and about being late, he picks up where he had left off the day before. He takes out some old yellowed press clippings on Crowley headed "The King of Depravity," "A Cannibal at Large," "The Worst Man in Britain," "The Wickedest Man in the World," and "A Man We'd Like to Hang." He explains that people have always loved to frighten themselves about Crowley and that Crowley got a huge kick out of encouraging this. Even now, he says, many local people drive the long way around the Loch to avoid passing in front of Boleskine and its supposedly evil influences. Eric assures us that such fears are nonsense and that Crowley was a scientist, a philosopher, a poet, and an altogether amusing man.

"Tell me," I say, because it is a question that Lee and I have pondered with more than passing curiosity, "did any of Crowley's scientific, poetic, and altogether amusing activities include putting hexes on people?"

Eric regards me quizzically a moment. "Crowley's philosophy," he says finally, "was 'Do what thou wilt.' If you put a hex on somebody, you'd be infringing on their wilt."

"I see," I say, relieved in no meaningful way.

Eric decides to show us some of his magical books, and as he's passing them around, a blonde two-year-old girl wanders into the room and tries to distract our attention by flirting wetly with us. I note that she exudes a terrible odor, and in time even Eric is forced to acknowledge this fact. "Uraina," he says, "I think your pants are full." As no apparent pants-emptying action follows this observation, I soon deduce that it has been made more in the spirit of pure research than of applied science.

Uraina fails to appreciate that her full pants have considerably diminished her charm and continues to flirt with us. This includes presenting us with her rag doll, her doily, her pencil, her matchbox, her magnifying glass, her coloring book, her ring, her compass, and it also includes conning Lee out of his watch and drawing on my shirt with a ballpoint pen. I am reluctant to make a fuss, perhaps fearing that to do so would be to risk being turned into a tadpole.

In one of Eric's magical books I spot a Hebrew word, *emet*. I ask Eric if he knows what it means. He doesn't.

"*Emet* means 'Truth,' " I say.

"Oh yeah?" says Eric. "Far out."

In another magical book of his I see the words *Adonai Ha-aretz*. I ask him if he knows what they mean. He says the words aloud, mispronouncing them. I correct his pronunciation and tell him they mean "God of the Earth."

"Oh yeah?" says Eric. "Far out. Hey," he says, "are you a student of the Kabbalah?"

"No," I say, "but I *was* a student in Hebrew school for ten years, and I have a pretty fair working knowledge of the language."

"Oh yeah?" says Eric. "Far out."

It soon becomes apparent to me that Eric's black magical books are peppered with Hebrew letters and names, and that every letter has been assigned a magical numerical value. I recall that *chai*, the Hebrew word for "life," has a numerical value of eighteen and I point this out to Eric.

"Oh yeah?" says Eric. "Far *out*."

Lee admits that he has spent six years in Hebrew school himself, and Eric finds that far out as well. I start figuring out what the numerical value of Eric's name would be in Hebrew, and soon we are all lying on the moth-eaten carpet, figuring out the magical numerical value of everybody's name from Crowley to Uraina. I have come to the spooky home of a black magician to learn Dark Secrets and I have ended up lying on his floor, giving him Hebrew lessons. It is not quite what my mother had in mind when she convinced me so many years ago that a knowledge of Hebrew would come in handy, but it is obviously the one thing that could have turned Eric on to us; from the frequency of Eric's "far-*outs*," it is clear that he is hooked. I exchange glances with Lee and he nods: This is the moment to tell Eric what we want from him.

"What we were thinking," I say to Eric, "is that we are both so interested in Crowley and in black magic that maybe you could show us something—something tangible—to encourage us to pursue the study of black magic ourselves."

"What kind of thing do y'all want me to show you?" says Eric carefully.

"Well," I say, "what have you got? I mean what kind of, you know, observable phenomena could you produce for us?"

Eric scratches his head and thinks this over.

"Gosh," he says finally, "about the only thing I can think of would be maybe to evoke some demons for y'all."

I look quickly at Lee and we try to conceal our glee.

"I think evoking some demons for us would be swell," I say. "How do we go about it?"

Eric takes down a book from his shelf entitled *The Lesser Key of Solomon, Goetia*, subheaded *The Book of Evil Spirits*.

"Take this book home with y'all tonight," says Eric. "It describes the various demons we could evoke, and it tells what we have to do in order to evoke them. Y'all study this and pick out a spirit you want to evoke, and then we'll get to work."

"Have you ever evoked any demons before?" I say.

"Only once," says Eric. "It was several years ago, and I didn't really know what I was doing, so all I evoked was a whirling white light that answered questions."

"I think we'd settle for that if we had to," I say.

DARKNESS has fallen on Boleskine, and since we are all going to be evoking together, I magnanimously ask Eric if he and his wife Iris would like to be our guests at dinner. Eric says far out, rounds up Iris and (I should have foreseen it) Uraina, and we make our way out of the house and into the moonlit night to the car, avoiding a couple of sheep and a goat and their collective droppings.

Eric is in high spirits and confides to us that Boleskine was built on the site of a church that an arsonist had burned to the ground after trapping the congregation inside it. For some reason, says Eric, ever since then Boleskine has been a source of doom for its owners: A general was one of the first folks to buy Boleskine, and he committed suicide by shooting himself through the head, his widow went mad and also came to a dreadful end, and so on.

"Did you tell them about Lord Fraser?" says Iris.

"No," says Eric. "They say that Lord Fraser, who was beheaded in the eighteenth century and who's buried in the Boleskine graveyard, rolls his head down the hallways of Boleskine at night."

"Have you ever heard him do it?" says Lee.

"Oh sure," says Eric. "But then I turn on the light, and there's never anything there."

And a good thing too, I think to myself as we get into the car and head out of the parking lot.

"That over there is the piggery," says Eric, pointing to one of the outbuildings. "One of the previous owners of Boleskine had this great get-rich-quick idea: He bought a whole lot of pigs and got people to invest in pig futures. He convinced them they were really going to make a fortune when he took the pigs to market. But he sort of over-subscribed on investments and so one day he locked the pigs in the piggery and split. Well, the pigs were soon starving to death and they turned cannibal. They started eating each other, and after a while those that were left died and rotted and festered. It was sort of a local scandal, and it took the next owner a pretty long time just to get rid of the smell."

A cheery story to whet our appetites for dinner. I drive past the piggery and pick up the public road that runs around the Loch. As we pass Boleskine graveyard, Lee observes that there is a full moon out tonight and wonders if there's anything going on in the graveyard at such times.

"Well," says Eric, "years ago a mother came here with her son who'd just gotten out of an insane asylum. They came to put flowers on the father's grave. Anyway, the kid had a sudden fit of madness and dashed his mother's brains out on the father's headstone. They say that every so often the mother crawls out of her grave and scratches around on her husband's headstone, trying to find her brains."

Dinner is at a country inn scarcely forty minutes up the road. Uraina tires of the event before even finishing her aperitif and goes into a series of numbers including crying, whining, screaming at the top of her lungs, and throwing various objects from our table onto the floor. Eric and Iris pretend not to notice, but Uraina manages to clear out the entire dining hall in less than a quarter of an hour.

By the time we drop Eric and Iris and Uraina off at Boleskine my nervous system is shot. And yet, as we drive back past Boleskine graveyard, a perverse idea for someone with a shot nervous system presents itself.

"Listen, Lee," I say, "do you think you have the guts to walk through Boleskine graveyard now? What with the full moon and everything, there's a remote chance we might see something."

Lee thinks awhile and finally decides that if *I'm* brave enough, then so is he. Besides, I have already decided to write an article about all of this, and I figure a walk through Boleskine graveyard ought to be good for a page or two. We park the car about fifty yards down the road and shut off the lights. For some insane reason I consider leaving the motor running for emergencies, but after a brief discussion, Lee and I reason that if we get into any trouble in the graveyard, we are never going to be able to make it as far as the car anyway.

We turn off the motor, get out of the car, and start walking very slowly back toward the graveyard. The moon has bleached the countryside a ghostly white color, and just beyond the graveyard, we can see Loch Ness shimmering brightly, holding God knows what kind of monsters. It is very chilly and I zip up my black leather motorcycle jacket. For no reason I can explain, I take my Swiss Army knife out of my pocket and open the largest blade.

"You think a Swiss Army knife is going to do you any good if we see Lord Fraser rolling his head around," says Lee, "or that lady scratching around for her brains?"

"No," I say, "it just makes me feel better to have it out."

We have reached the rusty ornate iron gate of the graveyard. We pause before entering.

"Maybe we should've brought along a crucifix," he says. "And a *mogen david*, just to be on the safe side."

"You think we're going to see anything?" I say.

"I don't know," he says. "Loch Ness is a really weird place. I guess anything's possible here."

"I can't figure out," I say, "whether I want to see something or not. I mean if we don't I'll be disappointed, and if we do I might be, uh, dead."

Swiss Army knife out ahead of me, crouched as if ready for a street fight, I open the iron gate and we enter Boleskine graveyard. My heart is hammering away hard in my chest.

"You scared?" I whisper to Lee.

"Nah. You?"

"Nah. Not that much."

I note that Lee is also in a street fighter's crouch. Two Jewish kids ready for a street fight with ghosts in a Scottish cemetery. We walk slowly down between the graves, heads swivelling back and forth like radar antennae. So far, I note, nothing has happened. We are in a very scary graveyard in a very scary area and so far nothing has happened. Soon we have walked the entire length of the graveyard and still nothing has happened.

"You know what this is?" I say. "Anticlimactic."

"I know," says Lee, "it's really boring. No ghosts, no zombies, not even a fresh cadaver."

I look over toward a walled compound that Eric had pointed out to us as being the place where Lord Fraser and his head were buried. It seems the only really sinister thing left in the graveyard.

"You want to go check out Lord Fraser's grave?" I say.

"Sure," says Lee.

We walk inside the Fraser compound and the shadows from the walls form spooky shapes on the ground. It is much scarier being inside the walled compound. There is much less chance of escape if something were to . . . materialize. I realize I am holding my breath so as to be able to hear the first sound of something dreadful if it should appear. We pause at a weathered headstone and I squat down to read what it says. It says: "Simon, 12th Lord Fraser of Lovat, Beheaded on Tower Hill, 1747."

I straighten up.

"Well, this is it," I say. "This is their last chance to pull something."

We look around expectantly. We hear and see nothing. We shrug and walk across the compound and through the exit to the other side of the wall. Still nothing.

"Well, Lord Fraser," I say, "you blew it. Right, Lee? He had his chance to show us something and he blew it, right?"

No reply from Lee. I turn around. Lee is gone.

Maybe Lord Fraser hasn't blown it after all. Maybe something dreadful has happened, I think. How do I feel about it? I am scared out of my skivvies, that's how I feel. I know it's good for the piece I'm writing, though. Assuming I live to write it, that is. Bad for me, good for the piece.

Probably nothing dreadful has happened at all. Probably good old Lee is just trying to scare me. Maybe old Lord Fraser showed up and made off with Lee, though—that's always a possibility, of course. But more likely, good old Lee is just trying to scare me. In either case, the best thing to do is shut up and wait.

Holding the Swiss Army knife ahead of me, I quietly flatten myself out along the wall of the Fraser compound and begin to wait. On the other side of the wall someone else is waiting too—either good old Lee or good old Lord Fraser. I will know which it is when he comes out. The one without the head will be Lord Fraser.

Suddenly a voice from inside the compound: "Hey, Dan?"

I recognize the voice—it's not Lord Fraser. I decide not to answer.

"Hey, Dan? I did a bad thing, buddy, I tried to scare ya. I don't think I want to be in here anymore, but I don't want you to do anything creepy when I come out, O.K.? O.K., buddy?"

I can't think of any particular reason to answer, so I don't.

After a while, very slowly and very cautiously, Lee comes out of the Fraser compound.

"Hello, Lee," I say.

The Lesser Key of Solomon describes seventy-two demons and the kinds of things they can be persuaded to do for you if you evoke them properly. Some can bring you wealth, some can make you invisible, but the demon that Lee and I like best is a guy named Sitri:

> **Sitri:** The Twelfth Spirit is Sitri. He is a Great Prince and appeareth at first with a Leopard's head and the wings of a Gryphon, but after the command of the Master of the Exorcism he putteth on Human shape, and that very beautiful. He enflameth Men with Women's love, and Women with Men's love; and causeth them also to show themselves naked if it be desired.
>
> —*The Lesser Key of Solomon*

We tell Eric we have decided to evoke Sitri. Eric says fine. What we must do next is find a shop that sells incense. There is an incense for every letter of the alphabet, he says, and we must get those that spell out Sitri's name so that we can burn them at the evocation. In the meantime, says Eric, we must practice chanting the evocations to Sitri aloud. We won't be able to evoke him without the incense, but, he says, "You'll feel exalted." I ask Eric for the location of a store that sells incense. Actually, says Eric, he doesn't happen to know of any—he's a stranger here himself.

Lee and I make a few self-conscious inquiries in Drumnadrochit about stores that sell incense, and we get nowhere. We make a few self-conscious stabs at chanting the evocations and we don't even feel exalted. We reassure each other that when we have the proper incense and we are actually in Crowley's temple with Eric, it will be a whole new ball game.

"You know what would really be great?" says Lee. "We finally get into the temple, with the incense and everything else, and Eric rolls up a newspaper into a cone and pours a pitcher of milk into it. And Iris comes out in a sequinned bathing suit and does card tricks."

I come across a passage in *The Lesser Key of Solomon* which worries me and I read it aloud to Lee:

It is curious to note the contrast between the noble means and the apparently vile ends of magical rituals. The latter are disguises for sublime truths. To destroy our enemies is to realize the illusion of duality, to excite compassion.

"Listen," says Lee, "just for the record, it was *you* who made the dumb joke about Eric pouring the pitcher of milk into the rolled-up newspaper."

WE DRIVE into the town of Inverness, half an hour away, and have no success with incense there either. We call Eric and ask him what to do. He says never mind the incense and never mind *The Lesser Key of Solomon*—he has decided that as long as we're doing this we might as well do a much more powerful evocation, the one described in *The Golden Dawn*. I don't know anything about *The Golden Dawn*, but it certainly *sounds* more powerful than any *lesser* key of anybody. For the *Golden Dawn* evocation, says Eric, we won't need incense, but we will need some other things. Like what?

"Y'all got a pencil and paper?" says Eric. "I'll read you a list."

"Go ahead," I say.

"First of all," says Eric, "we'll need a magical sword, a magical chalice, a magical dagger, and two nefolite robes."

"Nefolite?" I say. "How do you spell that?"

I figure nefolite is some terrific magical substance like, I don't know, kryptonite.

"Let me check the book," says Eric. "Oh yeah, here it is. Nefolite: N-E-O-P-H-Y-T-E."

"Uh, that spells *neophyte*," I say. "Is that what you mean, Eric, *neophyte*?"

"Yeah," he says, "that's it—nefolite."

"O.K.," I say, confidence in Eric running out of me like sand out of a nefolite egg-timer. "Where do we get all this stuff?"

"I called a friend of mine in Atlanta last night to find out if he knew of any magical supply houses that y'all could order from, and the only one he knows of is in London. The guy's name is George Alexander, and here's his number." Eric reads me a phone number in London. "Just tell him," says Eric, "that you'd like to order a magical sword, a magical chalice, and a magical dagger according to Golden Dawn specifications. He'll know what that means. I think I know a place where I can get y'all two nefolite robes."

I say O.K. and hang up and call the number in London. Soon I am talking to George Alexander, a very pleasant man with a cockney accent.

"Uh, a couple of friends of mine and I are going to have this evocation," I say, "and what we'd like to order from you is, uh, a magical sword, a magical chalice, and a magical dagger according to Golden Dawn specifications."

"According to *which* Golden Dawn specifications?" says George Alexander.

"Uh . . . this guy said you'd know what that meant," I say lamely.

"There are quite a few Golden Dawn specifications," says George Alexander. "I'll need to know which ones you want."

"I see," I say. "O.K., I'll find out and call you back."

I call Eric and tell him it's not enough to just say according to Golden Dawn specifications and Eric seems irked. I convince Eric to call George Alexander himself and get it all squared away. Eric agrees and says there's a couple more things he's got for my list: an oak disc, four tin discs, a magical wand, two magical pillars, four magical flashing tablets, two magical banners, and an altar made of cedar wood. He gives me the dimensions for the things we have to build and tells me to get back to him as soon as we've bought the raw materials—we should start with the cedar wood for the altar.

I hang up and show Lee the dishearteningly long list of things we need.

"Why can't Eric just twink his nose like Samantha on *Bewitched?*" says Lee.

WE HAVE gone to the only three lumberyards in Inverness, and none of them has any cedar. We are directed to a place outside of Inverness, and that place does have cedar, but they are too busy to cut it for us. We are told to come back in a few days.

We go back to Inverness to buy brushes and paints to make the flashing tablets. The flashing tablets are four wooden boards twenty-six inches by twenty-six inches, Eric has told me, that correspond to the four elements—earth, air, fire, and water. The earth tablet is to be painted black and white, the air tablet yellow and white, the fire tablet red and white, the water tablet blue and white. The tablets are then to be lettered with a series of secret letters within squares to spell out secret names of spirits. Eric has the diagrams for the painting and lettering in his Golden Dawn books at Boleskine.

Having been an art major in college, I figure I know what I am doing when it comes to painting. I am wrong. When I was an art major in college I was always too eager to get started and too lazy to begin things properly. I was too impatient to put down enough newspapers to protect the floor. I was too impatient to put on two coats of primer if I thought I could get away with one. Well, folks, I'm here to tell you that what we were too impatient to do in college we are too impatient to do in real life. Assuming that constructing magical flashing tablets to evoke evil spirits is real life.

So what Lee and I do is we put one coat of primer on the boards when we should be putting on two, and we paint them with spray enamel on the cement floor of my hotel room terrace without putting down enough newspapers. And so the paint refuses to adhere to the boards, and there are now squarish outlines of sprayed color on my terrace floor. I will solve the latter problem, I decide, by getting some aerosol cans of gray enamel and spraying over the squarish outlines on the terrace.

Eric has given his favorite Golden Dawn specifications to George Alexander and I have sent George Alexander a bank draft for £39 (or $97.50) for sword, chalice, and dagger. And so we are ineptly and expensively on our magical way.

Because the boards haven't been primed properly we have to strip off the paint and start over. Lee and I have begun dividing our time between driving to Inverness for supplies and sitting in my hotel room painting. To complicate things, Eric has given us the wrong proportions for the flashing tablets, so we have to take them back to the lumberyard to be recut, and then reprime and repaint them yet again. We have also begun work on the two magical banners—the banner of the east and the banner of the west—which we are fashioning out of silk, satin ribbon, and huge swatches of industrial nylon.

"The things you have to go through to see a naked lady these days," says Lee.

Every so often Lee and I pause in our magical work and ask ourselves what the hell we are doing and why the hell we are doing it. The answer we always come up with is that it may be crazy and we may be wasting our time (and my money),

but what if black magic really works? And then we start working again.

WE ARE at Boleskine, studying the elaborate
instructions in the Golden Dawn books for lettering the flashing tablets. Eric says I can either letter them in English or in
Enochian. I ask what Enochian is. It's the Angelic language,
Eric says. I ask where we got the Enochian alphabet. From
the Angels, he says. It is clear Eric means the winged rather
than the motorcycled variety of Angels. How did the Angels
teach us their alphabet? I ask. Well, says Eric, Angels don't
speak, but they have on occasions in the past taught us their
alphabet by first pointing to a letter in our alphabet, then
pointing to one in theirs, and so on. I look at a sample of the
Enochian alphabet in the Golden Dawn books and it is immediately clear to me that only a certified Angel would have
the patience to letter even so much as a note to the milkman
in Enochian. Eric reluctantly agrees to let me letter the flashing tablets in English.

Uraina is once more in our midst, flirting wetly with us,
her pants once more full, or perhaps unchanged from the last
time.

I ask Iris what it's like to be a black magician's wife. Iris
says she's not at all interested in black magic, although she has
occasionally seen its practicality.

"Like this time these three spirits showed up at the door,"
she says. "Eric and I were in bed and suddenly I felt this very
creepy feeling. This feeling of dread that was so terrible I could
neither move nor speak. And then I see these three spirits
materialize at the door of our bedroom—a chick and two cats."

"What did the spirits look like?" I say.

"They were in human form," says Iris, "but they were sort
of gray and indefinite. And they were wearing black turtle-
necks. Anyway, the chick kind of kneels down and says in

this real creepy voice, 'Eric, there's someone here to see you.' I was completely paralyzed with fear. I couldn't move."

"What happened?" I say.

"Well," says Iris, "Eric had drawn his magic circle around the bedroom before he went to bed like he always does, so the spirits couldn't enter the bedroom. And then Eric performed a banishing ceremony, and that did it."

"That did what?" I say.

"Made them distintegrate," she says.

WE ARE driving Eric back from Inverness from yet another magical-supply-buying trip and we are chatting about Crowley's bisexuality and his curious sex practices and one thing and another, and Eric happens to mention that sex magic is the most powerful kind there is. We, being not wholly uninterested in the sexual aspects of magic, press Eric to elucidate.

"Well, for one thing," says Eric, "sex magic is the best way to magically charge a talisman."

"How do you charge a talisman with sex magic?" I say.

"By magical masturbation," says Eric.

There is a pause wherein Lee and I silently debate whether or not Eric is kidding. Finally we both realize that Eric never kids. It seems a delicate subject to pursue, and I try to do so as tactfully as possible. I ask Eric to explain the ritual of magical masturbation. He is evasive and uses a number of euphemisms I don't quite understand. I try very hard to think of the precise delicate phrasing that will unlock the secret.

"Are you saying," I ask, "that to magically charge the talisman you, uh, jerk off on it?"

Lee winces, Eric mumbles some sort of assent, and another magical mystery has been revealed to us.

Eric says that Crowley frequently charged talismans by means of magical masturbation. Crowley generally had no trouble seducing whatever woman or man he lusted after into various acts of magical sex. Once, however, he encountered a beautiful woman whom he wanted and who could not have been less interested in him. The more Crowley hungered after her, the more repulsive she found him. He thereupon magically charged a talisman and went out in pursuit of her.

"And she fell in a swoon at his feet?" I say hopefully.

"No," says Eric. "Every old hag in the town ran after him, and even the mules and donkeys, but the woman herself found him more repulsive than ever."

Lee and I chortle politely at the story. Then the chortle coagulates in my throat as a semi-magical realization passes over me: If Aleister Crowley, the hottest black magician of recent history, charges a talisman with the most powerful and messy magic there is and if all he gets for his efforts is having hags and mules and donkeys get horny for him, then what is going to happen when old nefolite Eric tries to evoke Sitri to show us naked ladies? Maybe Sitri will enable ladies to see *us* naked. Maybe Sitri will enable us to see *ourselves* naked. Maybe Sitri will enable us to see *him* naked. None of the above seem to justify the expenditure of $97.50 for magical sword, chalice, and dagger, nor the additional hundred or so bucks I've spent on other magical supplies, to say nothing of the hours both Lee and I have thus far put in on the magical banners and flashing tablets.

And yet, since we *have* invested so much time and money, how can we possibly stop short of our goal? What if there really *is* something to all this mystical gobbledygook? And if there isn't anything to it, why is it that every single person we've talked to up here, be they Scots, English, or Americans, has warned us to stay away from black magic and not to tamper with the unknown?

Since the Carys nearly kicked Lee off their property, we've been extremely careful not to let anybody know what we've been up to at Boleskine. But I haven't been able to resist mentioning to people I meet that we've been *thinking* of visiting Boleskine, just to get their reactions. A British member of the Loch Ness Investigation Bureau named Dick Raynor said to me: "You wouldn't climb into a high performance racing car and drive it with no knowledge of the controls, would you? Then why would you muck about with things you don't understand at Boleskine?" Holly Arnold, his American associate, had added ominously: "There are some things that should not be tampered with." At the hotel, I had said to a personable young Englishman named Steve Hearst, who is, I believe, a graduate of Cambridge, "If I told you I was thinking of going up to Boleskine and exploring, would you advise me not to?" "I would *ask* you not to," said Steve Hearst.

A PACKAGE arrives from the magical supply house in London. Inside is something that looks less like a magical chalice than a sort of budget kiddush cup. I can find no magical sword or dagger. I phone George Alexander in London. He says he mailed the sword and dagger at the same time as the chalice and they should be arriving shortly.

Eric informs us that he has to go to London for a few days to help Jimmy Page open up an occult bookstore. When he returns, we should be through making the flashing tablets and the magical banners, and so on. Also the sword and dagger should have arrived, and we will then be able to have our evocation. Eric will call us when he gets to London and tell us exactly what day to expect him back in Scotland for the evocation.

While Eric is gone, we work feverishly on the tablets and the banners, and we also do a bit of research on Crowley himself. The man certainly appears to have led a spunky life.

"This man Crowley," said an article in the London *Sunday Express* in 1923, "is one of the most sinister figures of modern times. He is a drug fiend, an author of vile books, the spreader of obscene practices. Yet such is his intellectual attainment and mental fascination that he is able to secure reputable publishers for his works and attract to him men and women of means and position."

Crowley's public behavior almost never went unnoticed. "He had," says his biographer and literary executor John Symonds, "some peculiar habits, that of giving women the Serpent's Kiss, for example, or of defecating on the drawing room carpet or on the stairs of a friend's house." Symonds describes an encounter between Crowley, Isadora Duncan, and her friend Mrs. Madeleine B. at a sidewalk café in Montparnasse: Crowley, dressed in sky-blue knickerbocker suit and matching beret and walking stick, "came over and was introduced to Mrs. B. As he took her hand, he said, 'May I give you the Serpent's Kiss?' He did not wait for an answer, raised her wrist to his mouth and bit the flesh between two teeth which, it was said, he had especially filed for that purpose; he drew blood and infected her."

Crowley was an excellent mountain climber and an alleged cannibal. "On one solitary mountain climbing expedition," says an article in the London *Sunday Express* in 1923, "it is actually affirmed that running short of provisions, he killed two of his native carriers, and *cut them up for food!* This incredible piece of cannibalism is cynically authenticated by 'The Beast' himself."

Such accusations amused Crowley and baffled his apologists. In *The Legend of Aleister Crowley* one of his followers comments on the above incidents: "If the legend is true, or even partially true; if he has killed and eaten only one coolie in the Himalayas, for example, instead of the two alleged; it will be my painful duty to bring him to justice, poet or no poet, if I can, lest he eat me."

I like the "if I can." I *love* the "lest he eat me." It seems that Crowley produced profound feelings of dread even in his admirers. And small wonder. Rumors aside, if you were only to read what Crowley *himself* wrote about his doings, it would scare the wee-wee out of you. For example, this charming tidbit on the art of magical sacrifice from Crowley's book, *Magick in Theory and Practice*:

> Those magicians who object to the use of blood have endeavored to replace it with incense. . . . But the bloody sacrifice, though dangerous, is more efficacious; and for nearly all purposes human sacrifice is the best. . . . A male child of perfect innocence and high intelligence is the most satisfactory and suitable victim. . . . It appears from the Magical Records of Frater Perdurabo [Crowley's magical name when speaking of himself in the third person] that He made this particular sacrifice on an average about one hundred fifty times every year. . . .

"Listen," says Lee, "what if Crowley really was as evil as he says? Eric is Crowley's *disciple*, right? What if Eric is as evil as Crowley? I mean maybe we're getting in over our heads here. Maybe we're really in danger."

ALTHOUGH the Japanese team I am supposed to be following as they hunt the Loch Ness Monster has in the three weeks I have been here done little more than hold press conferences to explain why they have thus far not started hunting, the hotel is crawling with journalists and TV film crews from all over the world. Once they get here and see that there is nothing to report, their eyes sort of glaze over and they begin wandering about, searching for some story, *any* story, to justify their being here.

I befriend NBC-TV News correspondent Liz Trotta and, deciding we can trust her, Lee and I tell her about our activities at Boleskine. She is fascinated. In fact she has heard that nearby Urquhart Castle, in ruins on the shore of the Loch for several centuries, is haunted by ghosts of brutally slaughtered Scottish clansmen. I propose a midnight visit. Urquhart Castle is a hundred yards from Lee's shack, and he's not excited about visiting neighborhood haunts, so Liz and I set off alone.

The way you get to Urquhart Castle is you park your car on the road that follows the Loch, then you walk down the steeply graded meadow till you reach the castle walls. As I turn off my headlights, we are plunged into total blackness. There are no street lights, no friendly lights from nearby houses, and no moon or stars out either because it is drizzling. I have brought along a penlight of dubious value, which flickers and goes out as we are scarcely more than twenty yards down the path to the castle.

Liz, who has been hanging around various foreign wars, nonchalantly getting shelled and shot at for years, is strangely terrified of what we might find in the castle. I am placed in the macho role of unruffled, courageous, and protective male, and as we continue descending the path, I wonder if there's the slightest chance of encountering anything dreadful. I mean if you can't come up with a single ghost at Boleskine graveyard during a full moon, what hope do you have at Urquhart Castle in a drizzle?

Every few steps we take, Liz stops, grabs my arm, and whispers "What was that?" I keep replying "What was *what?*" but it is beginning to take its toll on my nerves. With the penlight now totally useless and the rain coming down harder, we inch our way along the path in the darkness, hanging onto each other to keep from falling.

Suddenly Liz stops and grips my arm so tightly I fear she's severed an artery.

"What's wrong?" I whisper.

"There's something ahead of us in the path," she whispers. "Something white."

"Don't be silly," I say, and look where she is indicating.

There is indeed something ahead of us in the path. Something white.

"Listen," I whisper, "it's nothing to be afraid of. It's just a rock or a boulder or something."

"Then why is it moving?" she says.

She is right. It is moving. It is very definitely moving. Toward us. Well, this is it, then—what you miss at Boleskine graveyard you make up at Urquhart Castle. Bad for me, good for the piece. I hold my breath, waiting to find out what dreadful thing the white shape coming toward us in the dark is.

And then, as it is almost upon us, I know what it is. You know what it is?

"A *lamb*," I say out loud. "Liz, we have almost both had coronary occlusions from seeing a cute little white woolly *lamb*."

Perversely, I am disappointed.

THE magical sword and dagger have still not come in the mail. George Alexander begs us to be patient. Lee has temporarily moved into my hotel room to expedite our magical work.

It is late one night, and we are still slaving over the accursed flashing tablets. Although the boards have finally been properly primed, the enamel has stubbornly refused to dry, days after being applied. We are forced to remove the paint with turpentine and start all over yet again. Lee opens the sliding glass door to the terrace, closes it behind him, and begins spraying more enamel. When he attempts to open the door again to enter the room, he can't. The door has mysteriously jammed. We each tug at it, separately and together, cursing, but it doesn't budge. The terrace is too high up for Lee to jump from, and it is too cold to sleep on all night. The only alternative we can see is to go and wake the manager of the hotel and get him to pry open the door with special tools. We do not know how we are going to explain to him why Lee is locked out on the terrace at this hour nor why the terrace floor is sprayed with squarish shapes of different colors.

We keep tugging and cursing for another half hour and then, miraculously, for no better reason than the door's mysteriously locking, it opens. Have we just had a magical occurrence? Far out.

The next day we are still in my room working. I am lettering the air tablet and Lee is shaking up a can of blue enamel for the water tablet. Suddenly, the can of blue enamel slips out of Lee's hands and, as if in slow motion, the cover of it arcs lazily away like a Frisbee, and the can itself does a leisurely half-gainer and falls face downward on the beige wall-to-wall carpet. Lee and I stare in mute horror as blue enamel spreads jauntily over the carpet.

Lee is the first to speak. "And to think we were worried about paint on the terrace," he says.

We have a quart of turpentine for cleaning brushes. We pour it on the blue stain and begin to dab at it with a towel. The stain gets slightly paler, slightly larger. Lee runs out of the hotel to the gas station next door and returns with two gallons of paraffin, which is a sort of British kerosene. We systematically empty the two gallons of paraffin on the carpet, rubbing away at it with successive bath towels. The stain is now only a shade or two paler, but quite impressively larger. The fumes from the paraffin have made us dizzy, and as we stare at the horrid blue stain and the volcanolike pile of nine formerly white bath towels by now doomed to a life of blueness, we burst into hysterical laughter. We feel like Mickey Mouse as the Sorcerer's Apprentice in *Fantasia*, vainly trying to stop the brooms from splashing buckets of water on the magician's floor.

Lee foresees living the rest of his life being pursued from country to country by the owner of the hotel, Alec Farquhar. "One day when I'm a very old man," says Lee, "I'll come running around a corner in Budapest, and there'll be Alec Farquhar with a carpet in his arms."

We alternate between deep depression and insane giggling.

We consider a number of solutions to the problem. One is to buy more blue enamel and stain the whole carpet the same color. Another is to get some beige enamel, paint over the blue, and then do some fancy brushwork to match the intricate brown pattern. It is beginning to look as though this is the end of the flashing tablets and of our chance to evoke Sitri.

"At this point," says Lee, "I'd rather see a clean carpet than a naked lady."

That night we both have terrible nightmares. At eight the next morning the maids tap on the door to see if we're up. "I have the inexplicable feeling," Lee whispers, "that a definite presence is trying to get into the room."

We realize we can't let the maids see the carpet. Lee tells them I'm asleep. The maids return at nine and again at ten. Lee tells them I'm still asleep. They say they have to change the linens. Lee tells them we'll do it ourselves. They tell him to open the door so they can give him the clean sheets. He goes to the door, opens it about three inches, and pulls in the clean sheets. They ask for the dirty ones. He tells them to wait, closes the door, goes back to the beds, and starts stripping off the old sheets.

I ask him in a whisper how this fits with what he told them about my being asleep: Is he supposed to be changing the sheets around me while I doze or what?

Lee gives the maids our dirty sheets. What about our towels, they say. Our towels! Well, says Lee, our towels are really so clean that we don't need any new ones yet. They accept this and leave. A close call, but we must resolve the problem of the towels today. We simply cannot give them our nine blue ones, but if we don't we'll never get any clean ones.

A bold plan suggests itself. We wait till there is nobody about, then skulk out into the halls to the maids' supply closet. It's locked. We creep down the hallway, quietly jiggling doorknobs, trying to find an unlocked room. We are not above swiping clean towels from our unsuspecting fellow guests, but we find no unlocked rooms. And then we spot something almost as good—a heap of soiled towels that the maids have left at the end of the hall. Cackling fiendishly, we scoop up the dirty towels and race back to the room, having pulled off perhaps the most asinine heist in the annals of crime.

An hour later, we locate the maids and trade the contraband soiled towels for clean ones. The maids, who have taken to acting toward us in the cautious and overly polite way reserved for the mentally defective, do not question why our towels were too clean to trade an hour ago and too dirty now to keep till tomorrow. The head housekeeper mutters under her breath that she's never seen anything so strange in her entire thirteen years of hotel work.

Now what to do with the blue towels? Clearly, if they are found anywhere in the hotel it is not going to take the deductive powers of Scotland Yard to figure out who altered their hue. There is only one solution. We wrap the nine blue towels in large plastic bags and creep down to the car with them past Alec Farquhar and speed off down the highway. About five miles from the hotel, we find a public trash bin. Pausing to make sure Alec has not followed us, we swiftly dump the grisly packages like some dismembered torsos into the trash bin and then tear off down the road to Inverness.

In Inverness we buy the only two bottles of carpet cleaner in town and three cans of gray enamel to cover up the paint on the terrace. We have thus far bought thirty-seven cans of automotive spray enamel at the paint store in Inverness. The proprietor must think we are painting a convoy of trucks. We return to the hotel room. When we spray the gray enamel on the terrace floor we realize there is neither enough of it nor is it dark enough to match the cement. We will have to cover it over with black. We pour the two bottles of carpet cleaner on the rug. The stain does not get any lighter, but the chemical is so powerful it stretches the material and dissolves the glue holding the carpet to the floor. The carpet bulges up toward us like a large blue baggy blister.

Throughout all of the above mishugas, we have been dimly aware of two very disturbing facts: (1) The magical sword and dagger have definitely not shown up, nor are they going to; they are either lost in the mail or else they were never sent. (2) Eric, who was supposed to call us when he got to London and return to Loch Ness in three days, has done neither. It's been a week and a half now, and neither Barry nor Fiona know how to reach him. They have given us a phone number in London, but every time we try it we get a recording machine with the voice of no known person on it. We leave countless urgent messages for Eric with the recorded voice, but Eric never calls.

It gradually dawns on us that Eric has disappeared. We can't believe it. Here we are with an investment by now of maybe $300 and some two hundred man-hours of work, and all we've got to show for it is a cut-rate metal goblet, a baggy blue carpet, and a psychedelic terrace floor. On the one hand, how can I afford to leave till Eric returns and sets up our evocation? On the other hand, what is there to indicate that Eric will ever return at all?

I have been here well over three weeks and the Japanese hunt for the Loch Ness Monster is, if possible, even farther behind schedule than the American hunt for Sitri. It is clear I must leave. But if I do, who will keep the maids out of my hotel room?

I convince Lee we must take dramatic action. We are going to straighten up the room and the terrace floor as best we can, and then we are going to *invite* the maids in to clean the room. It's the only way we'll be able to tell how much trouble we're really in.

We wander through the hall till we find the maids. They

smile nervously at us and ask if we want to trade any more sheets or towels. No, we say, what we'd really like is for them to clean our room. They look alarmed. Clean the room? What, exactly, did we have in mind? A clean room, we say. Well, they'll have to get permission from the head housekeeper. Fine. We go out and come back and the room hasn't been touched. Will it be as hard to get them to come in now as it was to keep them out before?

Our need to find out how others view the carpet is becoming an obsession. We spot a guy we've gotten friendly with, a lovely Irish soundman from the NBC-TV film crew. We ask him into our room for a chat. He comes in. We hold our breath. He doesn't notice the carpet. He sits down. He doesn't notice the carpet. He asks what we want to chat about. I decide it is time to force the issue.

Looking at the carpet as if for the first time, I say, "What the hell is *that*?"

The Irish newsman looks at the carpet.

"What the hell is *what*?" he asks.

"*That*," I say, wanting to hear what he's going to find worse, the blue stain or the wrinkled bulge.

He bends down close to the spot we've been pouring gallons of liquid money onto for the past several days. He shrugs.

"I don't know," he says. "Looks like somebody spilled something there a long time ago."

Lee and I exchange relieved and joyous looks.

Later in the day the maids, under heavy guard, enter the room, find no dismembered bodies or bloody axes, and change the sheets and towels. We are not there to see it, and if they ever notice the abominations on the carpet and the terrace floor, they never mention it.

We are home free. And I am free to leave. I pack up my gear and drop Lee off at his drafty clapboard shack and I bid him a fond farewell.

"Well, Dorothy," says Lee, "I guess Kansas is going to seem pretty dull after this."

I AM back in New York and going through Customs at John F. Kennedy Airport, and I am feeling very frustrated that I do not have a really dramatic ending to my story. The Customs man looks through my suitcase with no particular interest, then glances at the large, flat rectangular package wrapped in brown paper that I am carrying.

"What's that," he says, "a painting?"

"No," I say, suddenly aware that I have one last chance to have an experience that would be bad for me but good for the piece. "It's black magical flashing tablets to be used in the evocation of evil spirits."

The Customs man is silent for several minutes. Nowhere in the training manual for Customs people does it prepare you to deal with the sort of statement I have just laid on him. It is clear that if I don't help him out he may never speak again.

"Want to take a look at them?" I say.

He is silent a moment longer. Finally he speaks.

"I would," he says. "But only out of my own curiosity."

As SOON as I get home I send Eric a long letter, telling him how much work we put in and how sad we were that it was all for nothing. I enclose color photos I have taken of the magical banners and the flashing tablets we have made. I saturate the letter with the magical, Kabbalistic, guilt-evoking phrases that the Jewish people have handed down from generation to generation. I know that Eric must answer my letter.

He does. Eagerly, I tear open Eric's letter. It's a five-pager. I begin to read:

"Dear Dan," it begins, "Do what thou wilt shall be the whole of the law." (Do you recall the *New Yorker* feature called "Letters We Never Finished Reading"?) I wade through several pages of equally appealing and chatty stuff from Eric. He begins by not apologizing for his disappearance, goes on to say that the sword and dagger getting lost in the mail were "right in line with the divination I had done which warned that this was not the proper time to begin such work." (P.S. The old sword and dagger were never found, but honest George sent me new ones.) Eric goes on to tell me, just as though there had never been any $300 or two hundred man-hours investment on our parts, a whole new list of things he wants me to do before we can have our evocation.

He continues: "Before I go any further with you on this matter I would like a proggress [sic] report on these instructions. This will strengthen your Aura and facilitate your spirit vision, and give me ample proof of your sencerity [sic] as true sceptic seeking only true ends."

He goes on to tell me some things he'd like me to send him "immediately." Then, in case I might somehow have missed the point, he adds: "Now before I conclude I wanted to make sure we are in agreement as to what becomes of the temple furnishings once we complete our work. In return for the use of the temple I suggest we leave the altar, banners, and tablets. The floor cloth and swords will be mine by right of concentration [sic?]. The robes and sigils for your self, will be yours. The perfumes we will split . . ." The letter is signed, informally as ever, "Love as the law, love under will, ERIC, Frater Binas Non Sunt of the outer A∴A∴."

ONE LAST postscript. I have recently met a clairvoyant from Holland who, astonishingly enough, has been able to prove to me that he has a number of very impressive and frightening powers. (More of him the next time we talk.) Anyway, as he happens to be something of an authority on occult matters, I thought to ask him his opinion of black magic.

"Black magic," said the clairvoyant in his thickish accent, "is phoney-baloney. You stick a needle in a doll of a man, of *course* he feels it. You don't need phoney-baloney dancing around and mumbo-jumbo. *Anybody* can do it—you don't need black magic."

Sleep well.

THE MORGUE

THE city morgue in New York is a fairly modern building right across the alley from the psycho ward of Bellevue Hospital at 30th Street and First Avenue. The morgue deals with all sudden, unnatural, and unattended deaths.

On the street floor of the morgue are ordinary offices. On the basement floor below is where they keep the bodies. Of the ninety thousand corpses a year that New York has to handle, about thirty thousand of them pass through this building. Seventy-five to eighty percent of these bodies have some sort of identification on them when they roll in. Roughly twenty-five percent of them are autopsied.

When a body is autopsied (or "postmortemed" or "posted"), the first step is to slice the scalp across the top of the head from ear to ear and roll the face right down like a rubber mask. Next, with an electric saw the top of the skull is cut off like the top of a jack-o-lantern, and the brain is taken out and dissected.

Then a deep Y-shaped incision is made in the torso, with the arms of the Y extending toward the shoulders and the base of the Y extending toward the groin. The flaps of skin are peeled back, and the abdominal cavity is opened up. A part of the rib cage must be removed with the electric saw in order to get at the heart and lungs. The heart, lungs, liver, kidneys, stomach, and intestines are lifted out, weighed, examined, and dissected, leaving the body a hollow shell.

Small samples of some of the organs are saved for examination under a microscope, along with a bit of blood and, occasionally, the contents of stomach and bladder.

The autopsy findings are dictated into the formal autopsy report by the doctor doing the autopsy, and the body is reassembled by a morgue attendant. In the New York City morgue, this job is usually done by an old crone nicknamed the Seamstress. She loosely stitches the skin of the corpse together with a long curved needle and a few yards of wet white twine, in the same loose overhand stitch you may have used to make moccasins from kits in summer camp.

When the corpse has been sewn back together, it is returned to its refrigerated numbered "box"—a sliding tray resembling a large filing-cabinet drawer. Bodies in the morgue are transported to and from their boxes on stainless-steel rolling carts known as "meat wagons."

The basement floor has blue-tiled walls and a double tier of stainless-steel boxes. The halls of the basement are kept spotlessly clean, but there is, nonetheless, the faint stench of rotting meat.

The reason I have come to the morgue on this chilly evening a few days before Christmas is to do research on a script I have been assigned to write. I have been brought here by two policemen—Sonny Grosso, who, with partner Eddie Egan, was one of the two cops who broke the famous French Connection heroin case, and Randy Jurgensen, who succeeded Eddie Egan as Sonny's partner when Egan left the job.

For a time, Sonny and Randy worked Homicide together, although Sonny is too squeamish to actually look directly at a corpse. How they handled that was Randy used to look at the corpse and dictate a description of it in a loud voice to Sonny, who took it all down in a little spiral-bound notebook in the next room.

Sonny's self-admitted squeamishness about corpses does not prevent him from taking great delight at the prospect of initiating me into the fraternity of those who have Seen the Dead.

"You aren't going to faint on us now, are ya, Dan?" says Sonny.

"I don't know," I say, because I truly don't.

"You'd be surprised how many cops faint at seeing their first stiff," says Sonny.

"Right," says Randy. "As a matter of fact, *lots* of men faint when they see a stiff. But no women do."

Sonny and Randy lead me downstairs to show me around, and we run into Dr. Michael Baden, the Medical Examiner. Baden is introduced to me, and I am treated to my first bona fide example of morgue humor.

"They bring a stiff in here yesterday," says Baden, grinning in anticipation. "I swear to God his shvantz is a foot long. One of the morgue men turns to me. 'Doc,' he says, 'I got a shvantz just like *this* guy's.' 'That long?' I say. 'Naw,' he says, 'that *dead*.'"

Sonny and Randy are on the floor with that one. I smile faintly, uncomfortable with the unexpectedly ghoulish tone the evening has taken on and dreading the confrontation with my first actual corpse, which I suspect is not long in coming.

"Well, Dan," says Baden with a wink at Sonny and Randy, "I suppose you're anxious to see something. Well now, what can I show you first? Anything in particular you're dying to see?"

I shake my head as Baden scans the cards attached to the fronts of the closest boxes, looking for something amusing.

"You like tattoos, Dan?" says Baden, grabbing a box handle

and pulling it open. The box, like a giant file drawer, slides toward us, revealing the naked body of a longish-haired blond man in his early twenties that is covered with ornate tattoos.

Well, there it is, I think, my first corpse. I do not faint. My first reaction is surprise that the corpse is (1) so lifelike and (2) not set up the way they are in the movies and on TV. In the movies and on TV if you saw a corpse in a morgue, it was covered with a sheet, and nothing peeked out at you but a pair of bare feet, which were the first thing out of the drawer, with a tag tied to one of the toes. In real life the head comes out first, as in birth, and there is no sheet—just the plain body, naked, with a few articles of clothing balled up at the feet.

I am amazed that the tattooed guy looks not dead but sleeping, as though he'd gotten a little hot and woozy and lain down for a fast nap in one of the refrigerated drawers and would any minute now stretch and yawn and put on his clothes.

"What about those tattoos, eh, Dan?" says Baden.

"How ya feeling, Dan?" says Sonny, who has been careful not to actually look at the corpse himself, giving me a poke in the ribs. "Not going to pass out on us, are ya?"

I shake my head. How I am feeling is not at all. The thought that I am looking at a young man who had probably not planned on lying here dead tonight and that it could very well be me in the drawer, with Baden pointing out some of my more amusing physical characteristics, is one that I have thus far managed to keep at a wholly intellectual level.

That, I decide, must be what makes Baden and the morgue attendants so relentlessly jocular about this ghastly place: They no longer look at a corpse and see themselves in the drawer. I'm terrified of catching my death of death, but they've been vaccinated. They've conquered death in some weird way; they somehow *own* it.

"What did this guy die of?" I say.

"Overdose. He was a junkie. See the tracks on his arms?"

Baden picks up one of the tattooed guy's arms, points out the track marks, then lets the dead limb drop to the drawer. It bounces as it hits. The gesture jars me. I had naively thought you treated the dead with respect, junkies or not.

"How come you can raise his arm?" is what I choose to say instead. "I mean I thought it would be stiff from rigor mortis."

"Stiffs aren't stiff for long," says Randy.

"Rigor mortis is a transitory condition," Baden explains.

"C'mon, Doc," says Sonny, "show us some others. Dan is getting bored here."

"Yeah, Doc," says Randy. "Dan wants to see some *women*. Right, Dan?"

"Sure," I say, "let's see some women."

"I've got a real honey here," says Baden with another wink, and slides out a tray containing a naked lady.

The naked lady is about sixty-five or seventy, with a huge fat hill of a stomach and collapsed breasts, a stern hawk's beak of a nose, and a dyed-blonde pompadour so well shellacked with hairspray that not one strand has fallen into disarray throughout the entire normally hair-mussing procedures of dropping dead and being carted off to the morgue and stripped of clothing and filed away under *D* for Dowager. There is potential here for a terrific hairspray commercial.

"How did this one die?" I say, dully aware that we could be looking at my own mother.

"Heart failure. She dropped dead right in the middle of Fifth Avenue. Right in front of Saks."

As we've been chatting and the Medical Examiner has been showing off his stock, various Black and Hispanic morgue workers have stopped, lingered briefly with smug, vaccinated smiles, then gone off about their favorite morgue activities. Now a new one, a white guy with a disquietingly depraved leer, has joined them for some fun.

"Let's see, what can I show you next?" says the M.E., looking around his showroom. "I know—we got a bunch of people in last night from a nightclub fire in the Village. Want to see some?"

"No!" I say too loudly as Baden begins sliding open another drawer, for suddenly it is beginning to get to me, a vague queasiness and an unsteadiness in my knees, and the thought of having to look at a horribly burned body—what some cops I know call a "roastie-toastie"—is more than I can bear just now.

"It's O.K.," says Baden with unexpected gentleness, "this gal wasn't burned at all—she died of smoke inhalation."

I allow myself a fast peek at the chunky middle-aged woman in the drawer, see a black face, and vaguely assume she's a Negro, then notice that she's white from the neck down. I am temporarily disoriented—perhaps she'd participated in some macabre minstrel show in the doomed nightclub?

"Their faces get black from the smoke," Baden explains, sensing my puzzlement.

"Hey, Doc," says the depraved-looking morgue man, "why don't you show them the torso?"

"The new torso or the old torso?" says Baden, sliding the black-faced woman out of sight.

"What's the difference between the new torso and the old torso?" I ask and am instantly aware that I don't wish to know the answer.

"The new torso has a chain wrapped around its penis," says the morgue man with a wet gleam in his eye. "The old torso's penis was chopped off with its limbs and head."

"Fag homicides," says Sonny. "The river's full of them."

"Yeah," says Randy, "you don't even find out about most floaters during the winter months. But the minute the warm weather sets in, the ripe ones start popping to the surface all over the place. My first corpse in Homicide was a floater. She was all puffed up like a balloon, and when we tried to fish her out of the river, she hit something sharp and burst. She exploded all over a brand-new sportscoat I'd just bought that day."

"That'll teach you to wear good clothes on the job," says Sonny.

We are ready to leave the morgue. The receiving doors at the far end of the hall open and a black morgue attendant enters, trundling a stainless-steel meat wagon ahead of him. On top of the meat wagon is something wrapped up in a green rubber sheet. Out of the end of the green rubber sheet is coming a thin red line of blood.

I am torn between a horrid fascination to see what it is that's wrapped up in the green rubber sheet and a deep yearning to turn away and beat it out of here.

What is wrapped up in the green rubber sheet is a "fresh one," the victim of a car crash. The morgue attendants pull out a drawer, slide up the meat wagon, and begin unwrapping the body. Sonny turns away, but I am unable to. The body is that of a man in his late fifties, and it is clad in comical-looking long underwear. The head is all wrapped up in sheets. As the morgue men unwrap the head, I finally turn away. At the instant I turn away, I hear Randy gasp.

"What happened?" I ask.

"The guy's head just came off," says Randy.

I start walking rapidly down the hall in the direction away from the body clad in comical long johns and no head. Sonny and Randy and the Medical Examiner fall in behind me, wanting to know if I'm all right, wanting to know if I want to stop off in the men's room to wash up. What I want most to do is to get the hell out of there, but I also feel a powerful urge to try to wash off the rancid film of death that feels like it's covering my skin.

We troop into the men's room, and I splash cold water on

my face and rub my closed eyelids and push the soap dispenser above the sink and cannot believe the slimy red gore that has plopped out into my hands.

Baden glances at my hands, then at my stricken face, and chuckles.

"That's iodine," he says. "We put it in with the soap to prevent infection."

We walk upstairs to find that a pre-Christmas party is in progress in one of the ground-floor offices. Twenty or thirty ordinary-looking clerical people are in the process of drinking ordinary vodka out of ordinary paper cups, joking and flirting with each other in an ordinary way, and dancing to ordinary, recorded Christmas carols only ten feet above the relentless awfulness of the floor below.

I walk shakily into the party, flash a plump secretary an uncertain smile, grab a bottle out of her hands, and gulp down six or seven gigantic swallows of vodka. Sonny and Randy and Baden explode with laughter and pound me on the back.

Hours later Sonny and Randy drop me off at my apartment. I triple-lock the door from the inside and turn on a light in the living room. Then I turn on a few more lights. Then I turn on every light in the apartment.

I decide it might be nice to hear some music, so I put a record on the stereo. Then I think it might also be nice to get the news, so I turn on the radio. Then I think it might be a little less lonely if the TV were playing too, and I turn it on as well. With all the lights on and all the sound, I crawl into bed with my clothes on. I manage to keep my eyes open till the sun comes up.

My *Playboy* editor and I are kicking around ideas I could write about. The talk turns to the kind of ads some folks run in the back of certain publications, inviting people to contact them for various sexual activities. My editor says, What would I think about following up some of these ads and writing about it?

I admit I've seen and fantasized about such ads but say I don't feel one has to do anything quite as rash as actually following up on them.

"Why not?" says my editor.

"Well," I say, "the whole area is kind of, you know, tacky, don't you think?"

"Sure," he says, "But not any more so than the orgy you wrote up for us."

I have to admit he has a point there. I confess the notion interests me, but I want to think it over awhile before I make my decision, one way or another. He says, "Take all the time you want."

I go out and buy a few publications that run sex ads. *Screw* and, for some reason, *The New York Review of Books* seem to be the best known of these. I find a number of ads that seem intriguing. For example:

Young high-school teacher. Can't make out with students—available for extracurricular activities after 3 p.m. Call Miss B. . . .

And:

Bad *señorita*. The meanest mother in town, and if you got the balls to come and see me, you will never forget me! I dare you to come! Call at once! . . .

Pretty conventional stuff, right? But then it gets a little kinkier. Like:

Mother & 19-year-old daughter will perform. Call Mrs. R. . . .

And:

Let me watch while you do your wife. No participation unless asked. Would also like to see two girls together. . . .

And:

Just like Mommy used to do—over my knee for a warm gratifying enema. Call Nurse Nancy. . . .

Or:

Why have you been disobedient? I am very upset with you. Call me *now*. Mistress Angela. . . .

Or, one of my favorites:

3 Militant Feminists. Young, brilliant and white, will bring your most unutterable ideas of humiliation into reality—and in front of two or three of us. We've waited a long time to do this, maybe you've waited a long time, too. By appointment only. . . .

My editor calls me in New York and asks if I've come to any decision. I say I'm still mulling it over. He says that if I stop mulling and start researching this tacky piece, not only will he pay me *Playboy*'s top rate for articles, but also he will respect me afterward. I tell him he has himself a deal.

I LOOK over the ads I have so far collected from *Screw* and *The New York Review of Books* and try to imagine meeting the advertisers. I can't quite envision myself over the knee of Nurse Nancy getting a warm gratifying enema; I can't recall disobeying Mistress Angela; I have trouble seeing my most unutterable ideas of humiliation brought to reality in front of the Three Militant Feminists; I have no wife to do while the anonymous advertiser of undesignated sex watches; and although I feel I have the balls to go and see the meanest mother in town, I'm not sure I *want* to. That leaves Miss B., the horny high-school teacher, and Mrs. R. and her nineteen-year-old performing daughter. I am very tempted by both of these offers, and yet I hesitate.

I think part of the problem is that I'm worried about what I'd do if Miss B. or Mrs. R. and her performing daughter turn out to be—how to put it?—nonbathers or serious fatties. I mean, I don't relish going into a situation where I have to either reject some nice but terribly unattractive person or else hop into the sack with her out of politeness.

And then I discover sex ads with photographs.

For between $3 and $3.50 a copy, you can buy on many newsstands in New York such publications as *Swingers Life*, *True Swingers*, *Mixer*, *The Seekers*, and *Girls Galore*. These publications have dispensed, in most cases, with such trivia as articles and stories and are totally comprised of several thousand ads for various forms of sex, all grouped by state or section of the country and almost all of them featuring photographs of the advertisers either nude or in one of a multitude of fetching stages of undress.

The photographs are mostly of women, who are mostly wearing either panties and no bras or black garter belts and stockings and boots and no panties. The nude ones sometimes have part of their faces or part of their vaginas inked over. (I would like to suggest to some doctoral candidate in psychology looking for a topic for a dissertation that he or she look into what makes some women ink out their faces in nude photos and others their vaginas.)

The women in these photographs range in age from perhaps sixteen to seventy-two and in attractiveness from dead ringers for Ernest Borgnine to ladies who could give Angie Dickinson a run for her money as queen of the hop. It is at first difficult for me to understand why ladies as gorgeous as the latter need to run *ads* in order to get schtupped. The reason becomes clearer to me as I go along.

I begin to have a very active fantasy life. Not your usual wham-bamb-thank-you-ma'am five-second fantasies, either. I select some advertiser in black garter belt and bush, posing against a wall of imitation pecky-cypress Weldwood paneling on which are hung the sort of little wrought-iron chotchkies that are considered chic in Red Bank, New Jersey. I stare into her face, which is wearing what she hopes is an expression of sexually sophisticated bemusement, but which is instead one of tragic vulnerability and longing for some hopelessly romantic figure she knows she hasn't a chance of meeting— some Red Bank version of Cary Grant with impeccable manners, an incredible foot-long rock-hard shvantz and even chicer wrought-iron chotchkies on his imitation pecky-cypress Weldwood paneling.

I sort of melt into the picture plane and am in the actual

room at the moment the badly lit photo is snapped. I explain to the startled quasi-nude lady that Cary Grant couldn't make it tonight but he has sent me instead and I am now going to lay on her forty perfect orgasms, total spiritual fulfillment, and dinner for two at Sardi's with a host of her favorite showbiz luminaries. The lady realizes the extent of her fantastic fortune, weeps for joy, and clasps me to her perky bosom.

I go through half a dozen magazines like this and select fifty or sixty of the best-looking women and most provocatively worded ads for people in the tri-state area. For example, a nude young honey with long straight hair to her tushy writes:

> N.Y.: I like the bizarre. Bi-minded & uninhibited. I've got plenty to give and can go forever. Can you match that? No sincere partner turned down. Send for my photo and you'll shout for joy. . . .

All ads with photos are signed with code numbers instead of names, and what you do is send your reply to the magazine, which then forwards it to the advertiser. The above ad is signed E-7036. I like the fact that E-7036 is bizarre, bi-minded and uninhibited, and can go forever. I make a note to send for E-7036's photo so I can shout with joy.

> N.J.: Well-built green-eyed auburn-haired nurse. Loves French culture, parties, couples, willing to meet pen pals. A college graduate, amusing Gloria has a 40″ bust.

I make definite plans to meet amusing Gloria and her forty-inch bust.

> Head bank teller, 22, enjoys dancing, get-togethers, quiet drives in the country and finer things in life. Wishes to meet sincere tall and short mature men. . . .

How should I come on with this lady—sincere-tall or short-mature? I'll try sincere-tall.

Attractive 54, seeks intelligent Jewish men or Navy men my age for dining and dancing. . . .

Since I won't be convincing as Navy and fifty-four, I'll try coming on intelligent and Jewish with this one.

In *Swingers Life* there are not one but three photos of a well-built, dark-haired smiling lady who writes:

Hot Syracuse, N.Y., housewife, 38-20-38, mid-20s, would like to meet and have sex with single men and love it. . . . Write to me for the best deep throat and straight sex you have ever had. I want to suck. I am hot. . . .

I admire this woman's directness and feel I have perhaps read her display ads on men's room walls. I shall write to her for the best deep throat and straight sex I have ever had, and I will, if absolutely necessary, even go to Syracuse to get it.

Talk about directness: how's this?

Very affectionate girl, 25, with attractive figure wants to hear from wealthy nudists. . . . Must show proof of wealth. . . .

Sprinkled among the predominantly female ads for men, women, and couples are occasional peculiar ads from men. Some are poignant and funny, like this:

Need well-endowed men to sleep with my wife. She is too horny for one man to handle. . . .

Some are mainly poignant. Like this one:

I am willing to meet a pretty woman that wears eyeglasses and single, the one who will go nude with just her eyeglasses on. . . .

And some reveal more than they intend. Like this guy, whose apparently unintentional error in wording betrays a strong need to reassure himself:

N.Y.: Good-looking white guy, 25, 5'10", would like to hear from passionate ladies in N.Y. Hurry. I won't be sorry. . . .

And then there are ads from ladies who sound so terrific that it seems almost unbearable to have to go through the whole lengthy process of writing to them in care of the magazine, having the magazine forward the letter to them, having them reply, and so on. Like this one:

Have plane, will travel. Sexy young vixen, 24, pilot, will fly any-where in U.S.A. and Canada for a meeting with interesting single men. . . .

Or this one:

N.J.: Terrific Puerto Rican twins: bi-minded, clean, healthy and young are seeking single men for 3-some thrills. If you are man enough to handle two great girls, we guarantee to deliver everything you want. . . .

With visions of sexy young vixen pilots and terrific, clean, healthy, young Puerto Rican twins dancing in my head, I mail off my first batch of letters. In them I describe myself accu-rately as thirty-eight, divorced, five-ten, one hundred and forty-five pounds, slender, strong, gentle, and willing to try anything that's fun, whether or not I've even heard of it before.

In each letter I enclose a picture of myself taken at a photo session in Las Vegas for the illustration of my orgy article in *Playboy*. In this picture I am naked and intertwined with about two dozen similarly nude showgirls and half a dozen chorus boys. The reason I send out this picture and not, say, my bar mitzvah picture is that it is, first of all, the only one I have of me nude, even though it doesn't actually show my penis, and secondly, I figure the proximity of all those terrific nude bodies will suggest that I am a lot more experienced a swinger than is indeed the case.

After a couple of weeks, the first replies start trickling in. Old Bizarre-Bi-minded-and-Uninhibited sends a rearview nude black-and-white Polaroid of herself with the following letter:

Dear Dan,

I'm so glad you answered my ad they say one picture is worth a thousand words so what better way for us to start communicating? Let's at least try!

I hope you'll want my other pictures, the black and white set is $7 and I have beautiful color for $13. I sincerely hope they'll prove to you that we speak the same language and I have the feeling that we do—so hurry up. I know you won't be disappointed.

What about you? What are you into in life? I would like to start an interesting correspondence but it takes *two*. Please write and be my other half.

Love,
Ellen J.

Hmmm. Well, the handwritten note in black ballpoint pen on orange stationery isn't the warmest personal letter I've ever received, but the enclosed picture is of a very pretty girl. Although I don't love being hustled to buy her pictures, I figure the girl has to make a living and, with the picture-selling out of the way, she'll then be free to go forever and make me shout with joy.

I send her the seven bucks in cash and tell her I'm anxious to meet her in person. I give her a brief rundown, since she asked, of what I'm into in life, including some adventures I've had recently while researching a book on the occult—taking part in a coven of teenage witches in Brooklyn, fooling around with black magic in Scotland, and participating in voodoo rites in Haiti. After all, she *did* say in her ad that she liked the bizarre, right?

The next letter I receive is from a blonde lady with a plain-ish face but a dynamite body. Along with a black-and-white rearview nude Polaroid of herself with the words "Hope you want to see the rest of me" scribbled on the back is the following letter:

Dear Dan,

This must be my day—really—had a bad night, but your letter brought the best out in me—and now, baby, all I really need is you to share it with.

Would you ever guess that I'm a belly dancer? Not *too* much class but a lot'a heart—and whatever else you see. I know my pics will prove that I know where it's at—and I hope it'll be where you're at.

I have color for $15—black and white for $8 and posters for $20—but I'm all Baubles, Bangles and Beads for you to play with. It's your Ball Park and my equipment—let's connect!

Playfully yours,
Genie M.

The letter from Playful Genie is at least a *little* more personal than the one from Ellen, what with the bad night she had and how my letter brought out the best in her and how she needs me to share it with and all. On the other hand, close inspection of the black ink in the body of the letter reveals it to be a photocopy. Quick question: Is it possible Playful Genie kept the original and sent me the Xerox? Or does she perhaps do mass mailings to hosts of guys named Dan?

I moisten a finger and rub it over the salutation. It smears.

Playful Genie Xeroxes her letters and pens in her salutations by hand. I take out Ellen's letter and submit it to the wet-finger test. Ellen is also revealed as a lady who Xeroxes letters and pens salutations.

Shades of the *Reader's Digest* subscription-renewal sweep-stakes: "Dear (name of subscriber): Imagine a brand-new $125,000 ranch house on (subscriber's street) with the name (subscriber's name) on the mailbox! . . ." Well, we always knew that the establishment was co-opting and ripping off the underground, but did we dream that the underground was co-opting and ripping off the establishment? That girls with good tits and tushes and Polaroid cameras were in the mail-order business with personal-letter techniques lifted bodily out of such bastions of establishmentarianism as Pleasantville, New York?

But wait a minute. Just because Ellen and Genie are trying to become direct-mail queens doesn't mean it's a universal practice. I mean, maybe Ellen and Genie are buddies and used to work together in the subscription department at *Reader's Digest* or Time-Life, dreaming the Great American Dream of striking out on their own and having their own little business. That hardly proves that the other four to five dozen lovelies I've written to are identically motivated, now, does it?

But, alas, a letter from Rosalie fails the wet-finger test. So does the letter from a young lady named Jennifer K. ($8 for black and white, $15 for color, $20 for both), as does the letter from a lady named Gabby G., who spares herself inking in salutations by beginning her letter "Hello My Love" ($7 black and white, $13 color), and one from Louise W., who wants $10—no checks, please—for "living expenses."

Well, six letters are certainly not enough to make a sweep-ing conclusion about the field, but it does seem the game is that these ladies at least get to sell you a few pics before they fork over their phone numbers. Is it worth it? Well, no, not to me, at any rate. On the other hand, I am on assignment to *Playboy*, and so it's not really *my* money I'm frittering away here. I send out the asked-for cash to each of the six ladies.

Letter number seven is the most direct so far. It is from a lady named Candy J. and it goes like so:

Dear Dan,

I'm very pleased that you answered my ad, and I think we may be compatable [*sic*]. If you can fit a 50 $ modeling fee in your budget I'll guarantee you a sexsational time! I am a master of erotic massage, and I love French. Call soon & we can make a date to meet at my Manhattan apt.

Sincerely,
Candy

I consider $50 a little steep until I get letter number eight from Trudy S., who tells me that although she's married, her husband "fully approves" of her activities and that *her* "modeling fee" is $100 for two hours.

I appreciate Trudy's and Candy's candor, but I feel that even old moneybags Hef doesn't need to bankroll me to a session with a professional hooker.

It is now obvious to me that I needn't expect a high percentage of meetings with the ladies so far contacted. It does make sense that, as I said before, no normally attractive woman is running sex ads because she is having trouble getting laid. If any of the mail-order photo sellers I've placed orders with come through for me with personal meetings, terrific. But I am clearly going to have to extend my base and respond to more than twenty advertisers.

I go back to the magazines. I begin to seek out the kinkier ads. The way I figure it, people with kinky sex hang-ups might find it harder to get the particular type of partners they need and might therefore have a higher proportion of sincerity than the girls in the mail-order Polaroid biz.

Submissive Miss loves to play "naughty girl in need of bare-bottomed spanking" to established mature (30–55) fatherly types who know how to pamper a paddled behind afterward. . . .

I don't know if I'd describe myself as a fatherly type, but I am certainly thirty to fifty-five and could probably figure out how to pamper a paddled behind if I had to.

Sensuous, passive, young woman loves to be bound & gagged. Will pose for erotic B&D photos. Loves to give Fr. culture, receive Greek culture. Versatile in all friendships. S/M of any type given or received. Your photo a must showing which of above desired. . . . Husband will, if desired, perform all of above. . . .

This may be the point where I should explain to you that when an advertiser says she loves to give "French culture" and receive "Greek culture," she does not mean that she will read aloud from Proust while you flash her photos of the Parthenon. What she means is that she digs putting your shvantz in both her mouth and her tushy. "Versatile" means not that she sculpts, does soft-shoe, and can replace the transmission in your Oldsmobile; it means that she is not averse to licking another lady's labia minora. "S/M" is, of course, sadomasochism. Except, I am told, on the West Coast, where it refers to slave/master sex. "B&D" is bondage and discipline. This means that the advertiser gets kicks out of one person being trussed up like a yearling calf while the other person does unspeakably tough and humiliating things to him like, I don't know, telling him he makes a lousy martini or needs to use Scope mouthwash.

Some advertisers say they like "TVs" and "water sports." This does not refer to *Eyewitness News* and the Australian crawl. TVs are transvestites—boys who wear Merry Widows and girls who wear—what? Jockstraps? And water sports is a euphemism for taking a leak on someone for romantic purposes. It is also known as "golden showers." (Listen, I hesitate to even mention it, but if you ever see an ad mentioning "hot lunches," I am told that is a euphemism for fresh B.M.s. What one does with *them* I leave to your own imagination.)

Now, did I mention that "parties" refer to orgies and that "English culture" refers to being whipped or spanked and that "animal training" means romantic idyls with a poodle, a police dog or a Lhasa Apso? I didn't think I had.

How do I know such things, you ask. Well, first of all, I'm a journalist who does his homework. And second, I've been around, cookie, I've been around.

Dominant girl likes submissive men, TVs, French performers. Especially those who will wear my undies. Super studs challenged & couples sending photos invited to watch or join. . . .

O.K., now you can read this ad and understand that the lady is not looking for Marcel Marceau to wear her undies on *Merv Griffin*. Aren't you glad I filled you in?

Submissive "tom-boy" type with very spankable bottom needs dominants who know how to control physical side, yet tease, humiliate & punish a semiwilling "slave" to ecstasy. Novice masters welcome. . . .

A fairly explicit ad, I think, and the photo accompanying it shows an attractive young lady bound with rope, as is usual in photos of masochistic advertisers. Although another terse, photoless ad in *Girls Galore* says only:

I have a large full round fat behind that I just love to have spanked with a heavy paddle.

The ad says nothing more, not even whether the large full round fat behind in question is attached to a male or a female person. Another ad, also photoless, in the same publication tends to give me the willies:

Topless model. Half one sex and half the other. I enjoy dating girls with long hair and tall gentlemen. . . .

I don't know if this person gets many responses to its ad. Certainly not from many girls possessing both long hair and tall gentlemen. Still, you never know.

In *Mixer,* I come across the best ad I have found to date. It shows five of the cutest young girls I have ever seen. They are standing on a beach, wearing bikinis on wonderful cute slender bodies and smiles on wonderful sweet beautiful faces. Here is what the copy says:

Sensuous group. Sensuous, slender, young stewardesses with great bodies, fascinated by B&D, would like to try it & other things. Will fly anywhere to meet men any age, dominant or submissive. We do not seek money, only fun! Penna. females.

Now, I ask you. Aren't they cutie pies? Do they sound like you'd want to do *everything* with them? Are they sincere? Who knows? But I abandon my usual short reply letter and write them a ridiculously long letter. I enclose not only my usual orgy photo but also a picture of me wearing a black-leather motorcycle jacket, sunglasses, a black cowboy hat, black-leather gloves with industrial zippers, and a gun belt. I figure this photo will let the sensuous stewardesses see another side of me, however inaccurate.

I send out about forty more letters, most of them to mas-ochists, sadists, and other weirdos. I haven't really decided if I will have the guts to become intimate with any of them, but it's sure fun to fantasize about.

In the meantime, I get further correspondence from our old friends Ellen, Genie, and Rosalie. Ellen sends me five black-and-white Polaroids in various split-beaver poses and a letter that says I'm her kind of man and that she doesn't want me to go away now, because she's "got photos that really show pink tit and pussy I know you would love." They'll cost me only $12 (a dollar price drop from the last letter), and this communication is signed "Suckingly, Ellen." Like her previous note, Ellen's suckingly signed letter is Xeroxed. So are the letters from Genie and Rosalie, which contain rela-tively demure pictures—only *one* split beaver in the bunch.

About this time, the first of the replies to the replies to the S/M ads start groveling and swaggering in. An authentically handwritten letter from a dominant lady in Cromwell, Con-necticut, named Virginia M. says that she can certainly give me the type of bondage and discipline I desire, that she has the proper equipment and experience and that she requires an advance "tribute-deposit" of at least $20. She guarantees full satisfaction and will arrange our first session when she receives the money.

A dominant lady in Albany, New York, named Joyce B. writes, in genuine handwriting on lined blue note paper, as follows:

Dear Slave:
   I require that all of my male slaves wear my lingerie. I request lots of tonguing up the asshole and licking and sucking along the crack. I require *much* cunnilingus—and all of this while I stand over you in the superior position. I require that all my slaves adore my naked body. If you are ready to *serve* and *obey,*

I will take off my lingerie and send them to you, but first you must send me $8 cash, for I cannot afford to give them away. I will also send complete directions and commands for you to follow while you are wearing them. I can then be assured if you are both submissive and obedient for that is the only type of slave I accept.

Your mistress,
Joyce

(Slave written at my dictation.)

P.S. For discretion—be sure to return this letter, and always send a stamped, addressed envelope if you want a reply.

Only a cynic would suspect that mistress Joyce was in the mail-order-undies biz, but since I have no immediate need for Joyce's pants, I hold off on whisking her my $8.

Two submissive ladies reply to my letters. One writes on the bottom of the note I mailed her:

Dear Dan—
Many thanks for answering the ad in *Swingers Life*. I appreciate your taking the time to answer; however, your letter and the photo hardly seem on target to my rather specific, and limited, areas of interest.

Her note is signed simply "B."

The second submissive miss sends a separate handwritten note to the same effect in teeny-weeny scrawl, signed "E."

Well, B. and E., I see I was wrong to send you my standard letter and photo instead of something more *macho*, a mistake that I shall correct immediately. I send both B. and E. copies of the picture of me in motorcycle jacket, shades, and cowboy hat. And, with different salutations, I answer both of them sternly in the following manner:

I can see that I was too nice to you in my previous letter. I am more than able to satisfy your specific needs. The enclosed photograph will show you a more accurate representation of my dominant personality than the group photo I sent you before.

It is clear to me that you must be punished for your insolence in assuming I could not satisfy your needs. Here, then, is what you will do:

Immediately upon receipt of this letter you will send me an apology by return mail. You will enclose your full name, address and phone number. I shall call you when it pleases me and I shall tell you when it will be convenient for me to see you.

You will then come over to my house and apologize in person and attempt to convince me not to punish you. As you are doing so, you will strip down to your panties. Your apology will not be accepted and you will be handcuffed and made to kneel on the floor with your buttocks in the air. I will then take down your panties and spank you until your naughty little cheeks are stinging hot with shame.

You will at this point be told to go into my bedroom, where I will strap your wrists and ankles into shackles and chain you to the bed. From then on, I shall do whatever I wish to you, and you will be forced to repeatedly satisfy me orally.

At such time as I have decided you've been punished enough to atone for your impudence, I will be kinder to you and will take care of you and show you as much tenderness as you seem to deserve.

I shall now close and await your reply. Remember, the longer you make me wait, the harder it will be on you.

> Dominantly,
> Dan Greenburg

P.S. In your reply, and in person, you may call me *Mr.* Greenburg.

I mail B. and E. copies of this letter before I have a chance to realize that I have undone myself with my closing sentence. If they are indeed masochists, then the warning that the longer they make me wait, the harder it will be on them can only *prolong* their procrastination. Ah, the pitfalls of the dominant role!

Three more letters from dominant dames arrive. The first is from one in New York City named Janet D. She sends me a short chatty handwritten note stapled to a much longer mimeographed letter, which I excerpt below:

> Suppose you were to meet in a private place a young woman of hatuer [sic] beauty, cruel and arrogant temperment [sic]. She orders you to strip completely, treats you as a chattel, spanks your bare-bottom very severely till your cheeks are blazing red. Then she makes you kneel before her and pay homage to her womanhood, sweet anus, bare-feet using only your mouth and tongue. To her you are simply a slave, an animal used to gain pleasure. Even when you finish pleasing her most private and sensual parts, she mocks you, perhaps whips you more cruelly, for bringing forth the weakness of her most beautiful flesh.
>
> Tell me if you dare how you'd react to this. If you are thrilled by the prospect of enslavement, perhaps I'll hear from you, with all I ask in this letter.
>
> Your most arrogant,
> Janet

I'll tell you, Janet, here's the thing: I won't deny that some of my sex fantasies have been of the submissive variety. There is something deliciously reminiscent of being the little boy again and having Mommy angry at one in a sexually titillating way. It is also very tempting to fantasize a situation where one has given up all control and any responsibility for whatever nasty sex things might develop—I mean, what could I *do*, Officer/Daddy/God/whoever, she overpowered me! Which, by the way, is the appeal of most submissive or rape fantasies, and we *all* have them from time to time, yes, indeedy.

But my problem, Janet, is this. First of all, I also have lots of fantasies where *I'm* the master and *I'm* barking out the sexual orders. As a matter of fact, about a year ago it was my practice the third or fourth time I went to bed with a lady to suggest it might be fun if I tied her up with a length of clothes-line and had my way with her. (Surprisingly few of them objected, by the way, and all who tried it admitted the experience was something of a turn-on.)

Second, and perhaps more important, my most arrogant Janet, how could I ever be thrilled by the prospect of enslavement for even twenty minutes to a woman who's a lousy speller? I mean "hatuer"? "temperment"? You can't be *serious*.

The second and third letters from dominant ladies are from Connie G. and Barbara R., both of New York, who are apparently into the S/M business in a big way. Along with their mimeographed letters, they send a number of items generally associated with serious mail-order solicitations.

First is a questionnaire of personal preferences in which I am asked to check whether I love, like, am unsure about, am indifferent toward or dislike a list of things including, in alphabetical order, Aggressive Women, Anal Adoration, Body Slavery, Bondage, Boots, Discipline (Mild), Discipline (Other), Equestrian Training (Woman Riding Man), Feet Bare & Beautiful, Female Authority, Fur (with Nudity), Foot Slavery & Service, Golden Showers, Leather, Lesbian Beauty & Authority, Man's Subjection to Woman as Destiny, Oral Adoration of Woman by Man (Reward), Oral Adoration of Woman by Prone Man (Forced), Punitive Women & Punishment, Submission (to Many Dominatrices), Submission (to One

Woman Only), S/M Demonstrations (Woman Above Man), Two Women Dominating One or More Men, Wrestling, etc., etc.

Let's see here, waiter—I think we'll have the Fur with Nudity to start, then the Feet Bare & Beautiful with a side order of Leather, then I think we'll try one order of Lesbian Beauty & Authority and, oh, yes, hold the Man's Subjection to Woman as Destiny, please.

Also sent by the ladies is literature describing a number of things one could get from them besides nasty treatment. For example, one could buy a cassette with thirty minutes of dominant palaver from Mistress Shirley at $12 a throw; or introductions to a gaggle of dominant colleagues of Mistress Connie at $3 apiece; or a set of bondage pics featuring Mistress Connie at $10 for six poses; or a Fetish Items Catalog at $2; or an estimate at $3 by Mistress Connie's Master Craftsmen (Mistress Craftspersons?) on any custom-made implement, rack, restraint or whatever your cowering little heart desires; or your choice of four stories written specially by Mistress Annette to satisfy any of four popular personal deviations, at $3 and $4 the story—we are told by Mistress Connie that Mistress Annette's stories, artwork and sense of humor are "truly Unsurpassable."

Samples of Mistress Annette's truly Unsurpassable stories, artwork and humor are enclosed, and I quote from two of them. From *Mistress of Pain*:

> "Alright, worm, you've proven you have an experienced tongue, but that hardly makes up for your insult. You will, however, be allowed to continue slave training. . . . The first rule you will remember is that you are never to rise above the level of my breasts," she said and lashed him across the back. . . . "The slightest infraction against any order I give will result in a severe whipping with this cat."

(Nobody better try whipping *me* with any cat, I can tell you that.)

Next is this from *Torture Unlimited*:

> When the doorbell finally rang Colleen was already fuming. Her new trainee was 20 minutes late for his first session, an unthinkable mistake. . . . He was only one among hundreds who had responded to her ad in the magazine. She yanked open the door and there he stood, head bowed. He began to stammer an apology, but she stopped him short with a vicious slap across his face. "There can be no excuse for this insult. You should have been kneeling at my steps at least an hour before you were due," she growled as she jerked him in the door and dragged him upstairs to her work-room.

Well, sir, if *that* doesn't prove Mistress Annette has an Unsurpassable sense of humor, I sure don't know what does. I make note of the dialog style for future use and then decide that Mistress Virginia's uncommercial and personal note is the only one I care to follow up on. I send her a check for $20 and await her response.

In the meantime, I get what looks like my first promise of an actual face-to-face contact: a typewritten note from someone named Kathy F.—"my real name," she says, leading me to wonder what false names she has given me previously. She urges me to telephone her and encloses a New York City phone number. There is no code letter or number on her letter, so I have no idea which advertiser she is. I am embarrassed to tell her this, in case she'd be offended to know that hers was not the only ad I answered, but I call her anyway.

Well, I needn't have been embarrassed about not knowing which one she is, because she clearly doesn't know which one I am, either.

"I'm the guy who sent you the group photo," I say. "I put an X on my chest so you'd know which one I was. Remember the picture?"

"No," she says. "Did you send me the ten dollars yet?"

"I don't know," I say. "I mean, I've sent a couple of girls ten dollars. I don't know if you were one of them. But how come you asked me to call you if you don't even know which one I am?"

"Well, I don't always send those notes out myself," she says. "I mean, sometimes the guy who handles my photos sends them out. How did you hear about me?"

"Through *Swingers Life*," I say.

This doesn't seem to ring a bell. I'm nonplussed. It's like when your phone rings and somebody's secretary asks if you'll hold for Mr. So-and-So and disappears and there you are holding a dead phone, waiting to talk to somebody you never asked to talk to in the first place.

Kathy asks me to tell her something about myself. I do. Then I ask her to tell me something about *herself*.

"Well," she says, "I work in a social-service agency nine to five right now, but it's just temporary, because I'm also going to college. I'm in sociology, although a lot of people have told me I have this really good voice and everything, so I was thinking of getting into acting or radio announcing."

As a matter of fact, Kathy's voice is nasal and New York-accented, so whoever told her she ought to go into announcing or acting had more up their sleeves than armpits. I ask if she wants to get together with me. She's evasive.

"I'm really new to the swinging scene, you know," she says.

"So am I," I say, delighted to find a fellow innocent.

"My pictures don't do me justice, either," she says. "I'm five-four and I weigh a hundred and twenty pounds, which you can't tell from my picture, and I have dark hair and green eyes."

"That sounds nice," I say.

"You know," she says, "mostly I'm a model. You know what that means?"

"Yes," I say. If you have to ask if someone knows what it means when you say you're a model, then you're not a model. You're a hooker.

"I mean, I still swing with guys I dig for free," she says, "but mostly I'm professional, or semipro. Until I either get my degree in soc. or break into the acting or announcing thing, I mean."

I ask her if she wants to get together so she can decide whether or not she digs me enough to swing with me for free, but she can't seem to decide even that. What with all these career decisions mucking up her head, I can hardly blame her. She finally says she'll come over for a drink after ten and will call first, although neither of these proves to be true.

I take out my swingers' magazines and try to figure out which one Kathy is by her description of herself. After scarcely an hour's detective work, I find her. The ad describes has as having dark hair and green eyes and the height and weight are the same as she told me on the phone. Kathy is revealed to be code number H-1018, who, at the time the ad was placed, lived in New Jersey.

I am quite proud of my detective work until I receive on the following day a note from the *real* H-1018 from deepest New Jersey, a person by the name of Pat.

Somewhat miffed, I return to my magazines but am still unable to come up with any other identity for Kathy than H-1018 in New Jersey. Since the note said Kathy was her *real* name, then perhaps Pat is her *fake* name?

It is getting far too complicated. But in running down further possible identities for Kathy, I discover something very interesting. I have become familiar enough with a hundred or so photos to discover that many advertisers change poses, add inked-on masks or G strings, and run several ads in the same publication. What they ask for in each ad may differ, but their physical descriptions and prose styles are often distinctive enough to identify the same person in several different ads. Sometimes the background details in their photos give them away—the same satin drapes with the one bad pleat, the same mosaic-patterned wallpaper with the identical brass chotchky.

I now see that I must have sent my seventy or eighty letters to only twenty or thirty ladies. Of course, the ladies themselves may not even realize this if, like Kathy, it's not they but some guy who is sending back their replies. Oh, it's beginning to sound very complicated, indeed.

More letters come in and, with them, opportunities to buy Polaroids of Crystal, Maria, Jan, Sharon, Natalie, Carla, Jennifer, Pat, Betty, Marianne, Selma, Beth, Jean, Jeannie, Mia, Carol, Joan, two Marys, and two Lindas. Also, it appears that at least one of my dominant ladyfriends has sold my name to a few S/M mailing lists, because I also receive offers to subscribe to three S/M magazines and invitations to attend an S/M mixer, an S/M ski party (where presumably you could have your leg broken without even getting to the slopes), and an S/M charter flight to Puerto Rico on which even the stewardesses and the flight crew are sadomasochists. ("Ladies and gentlemen, the captain has requested that you fasten your wrist and ankle shackles in preparation for take-off. We will be flying this afternoon at an altitude of thirty-five feet, and once aloft, your stewardesses will be serving a hot lunch.")

Certain things are becoming clear to me. Not every lady I have written to wants to sell me Polaroids, panties, or S/M software. Some—like Candy and Trudy—want to fuck me for money. Some—like Virginia and Louise—want to fuck me *out* of money. Because, although I sent Louise $10 dollars and Virginia $20, I never hear from either of them again. "Please do not reply that you do not wish to buy photos," said Louise's earnest letter, "that is not my objective." Well, *that's* cer-

tainly true. "I assure you I will keep my part of the bargain."
Right, Louise, baby.

The thing that is becoming clearest of all to me, however,
is that trying to get laid by answering sex ads is about twelve
times harder than by simply meeting a girl and taking her out
on a date. I'm not suggesting that *everybody* who advertises
in swingers' magazines is a phony, mind you. I wouldn't say
that's true of more than, oh, I don't know, 97 percent of them.

I have just about decided to chuck the whole experience
and get on to other things when a letter arrives from E. Remember old E.? Who thought I couldn't meet her specific
masochistic needs?

E. turns out to be Edith, who lives on the West Side of
New York City and who has changed her mind about my
ability to dominate her. She encloses her phone number and
implores me to call.

My phone call to Edith is short and to the point. My tone
of voice with her is quite stern. I make an appointment for
her to come to my house at eight the following night, and I
tell her not to wear panty hose. (I hate panty hose, in case
I haven't told you.) I tell her to wear panties, a garter belt,
and stockings. She says she understands.

I have undertaken a great responsibility. I must not fail this
person. I must dominate and persecute and humiliate her to
rival her wildest dreams. I will need a scenario. I will need
props.

Down the block from me is a store called The Pleasure
Chest. It is a store that sells all sorts of sexual props—vibrators, French ticklers, dildos—the usual stuff. What makes
this store unique is that it specializes in S/M devices, which
it custom-designs. Oh, you can buy your ordinary New York
Police Department regulation handcuffs there, sure, but you
can also buy chain shackles of black leather and steel for
wrists and ankles, heavy canvas straitjackets, black-leather

hoods with heavy industrial zippers, leather and steel body harnesses, whips and crops and quirts and gags and paddles to warm the cockles of the coldest sadomasochistic heart.

Knowing that a homely length of clothesline is never going to be enough for Edith, I lay out $8 for handcuffs and $25 each for two sets of wrist and ankle shackles. I suppose that going into an S/M store to buy chain shackles in the seventies is equivalent to going into a drugstore for a box of condoms in the fifties. I've done both with an equal amount of aplomb.

Back home, it occurs to me for the first time that I have no place to attach the swivel snaps on the ends of the shackles. If only I owned a four-poster bed. Luckily, I am handy with tools, and without much hassle I attach four screw eyes at strategic locations in the platform of the bed to anchor the swivel snaps. I practice snapping the snaps to the shackles and buckling and unbuckling the heavy leather straps so it will look like I've been doing it all my life.

IT IS the following evening. Normally, when I arrange to see a woman in the evening, I take her to dinner before or after whatever else we do, but this is not normally and I somehow feel that taking Edith to dinner would cause her or any other serious masochist to eye me with suspicion and even wonder whether I might not be a closet nice guy.

Besides, having to maintain a monolithic sadist role throughout an entire restaurant meal sounds positively draining. I'm not even sure how I'd go about it. I guess I could order the best things on the menu for myself and nothing for her. Or make her eat only those foods she has always despised. I could order half a grapefruit and mash it, Cagney-like, into her face. As I say, too draining. Well, I'll just heat up a can of ravioli at home after she leaves.

At seven-thirty, I begin to get ready. I lay out the wrist and ankle shackles and the handcuffs. I begin to dress.

I don't know how masochists generally prefer their beaux

to dress, but from the pictures I've seen, I'd say the touchstone was black leather and rubberwear. I have a black-rubber skin-diver's wet suit and flippers somewhere, which does seem a bit extreme, and I think I might still own a pair of galoshes. But that's about the extent of my rubberwear, and not really the macho image I'd had in mind.

I do own a pair of black-leather jeans. Although they are tight and confining and make me perspire and squeak when I walk, they are clearly the thing to wear tonight. I put them on, along with a pair of black-leather boots and a wide black belt with a heavy steel buckle.

The shirt is going to be a problem, as I have nothing very butch. I finally elect to wear my black motorcycle jacket instead of a shirt. It'll be warm, but what the hell—either you're a serious sadist or you're not. I put on my sunglasses and the room gets considerably dimmer, but the look, as I appraise myself in the mirror, is properly menacing and worth it.

In the photo I sent Edith, I wore all this, plus a black cowboy hat, zippered black gloves and a gun belt. I put on the hat and gloves and sling the gun belt over my shoulder, but it doesn't look quite right. Is it possible I'm beginning to overdo it? I take off the hat and gloves and gun belt. Still menacing, no doubt about it, but as menacing as before? I buckle the gun belt around my hips. Nice, but the empty holster looks funny. I take out an old Colt Peacemaker that I found in Mexico and rebuilt and I drop it into the holster. Better. I pull on the gloves again and leave them rakishly unzipped and plop the cowboy hat back on my head.

Hmmm. Very nice. Very ominous. I go into a gunfighter's crouch, left hand out, right hand poised above the Colt. Now a nasty sneer creeps over my lips. Perfect. It's Jack Palance in *Shane* with a quick stopover in *The Wild One* to become a Hell's Angel.

The doorbell rings, jarring me out of my sneer. I whip off gun belt, cowboy hat, and gloves and walk slowly to the door, considerably hampered by my cumbersome costume, creaking impressively from every fold of leather. I press the buzzer, amble into the hall and pose menacingly atop the steep flight of stairs as the door at the bottom swings inward.

An attractive young woman with dark hair, somewhat tough face, and possible Hebraic origins enters. She sees me framed above her in all my leather and appears badly startled. My inclination is to say "Hi, Edith," but guys wearing this much leather don't say "Hi, Edith."

"You're late," I snarl. Actually, she's exactly on time, but I can't think of anything else to say.

She starts to stammer an apology, but I cut her short with a vicious sneeze.

"There can be no excuse for this insult—you should have been kneeling at my steps at least an hour before you were due," I growl as I drag her upstairs to my workroom, thankful for Mistress Annette's scenario.

Upstairs, I look her over. Edith has an attractive if slightly hard face, as I said before. Her hair is black and on the short side. She is wearing a beige silk blouse, a delicate gold chain around her neck, a tan skirt, and tan shoes with high heels. She is swallowing a lot and looks really nervous. If a car backfired outside now, she'd leap about twelve feet in the air. I'd like to comfort her, but it would be out of character.

Usually, when people come to my house in the evening, I offer them a drink. I wonder if Edith would be disappointed by any evidence of hospitality. I decide to risk it.

"Would you like a drink?" I say.

She nods gratefully.

"What would you like."

"Anything," she says.

"How's about a gin and tonic?"

"Fine," she says. "Actually, *vodka* and tonic would be better. If you have it, I mean. And if it's not too much trouble."

"I have it," I say, "and it's not any more trouble than gin."

"Fine," she says.

I creak slowly over to the bar and prepare to make the drinks.

"If you have Stolichnaya, I'd prefer that," she says. "But if not, don't worry about it."

"I don't have Stolichnaya," I say.

"Fine," she says. "Don't worry about it."

I go back to making the drinks. I should have had Stolichnaya. I should have turned up both the lights and the air conditioner. With my sunglasses on in the dim bar light, I can barely make out bottles and glasses, and inside my jacket and leather pants, it is considerably muggier than out.

"If you happen to have a slice of lime, that would be ideal," she says. "But if not, don't worry about it."

I turn around and appraise her coolly.

"You certainly do have very specific requests for a submissive personality," I say. "I'm not sure I like that. Worm." (I don't know if I actually said worm, but I think I did.)

"I'm sorry," she says, "I don't know why I said that. I don't care about the lime if you don't have any, honestly I don't."

"Whether I have limes or not is beside the point," I say. "And I think the reason you asked was to test me."

She nods rapidly several times and swallows hard.

"I'm sure you're probably right," she says.

"That's another thing I can't stand," I say, "people who say 'I'm sure you're probably right.' Either you're *sure* I'm right or you're not. If it's only 'probably,' then you're not sure."

She nods even more rapidly and swallows hard again.

"I think I'm going to have to punish you for your impudence," I say. "Take off your skirt."

Her cheeks flush. To the extent that I am able to tell a flushed cheek from an unflushed one through my shades.

"You mean right now?" she says.

"I mean right now this instant."

She fumbles with the zipper on her skirt, unzips it, and starts to step out of it.

"Just a minute," I say. "Are you wearing *panty hose?*"

She gets more flustered and nods.

"Didn't I tell you on the phone I *hate* panty hose?"

"I must have misunderstood," she says. "I thought you said you wanted me to wear them."

"I specifically told you not to wear them," I say. "Take everything off but your panties and kneel on the floor."

"What are you going to do to me?" she says apprehensively but with obvious excitement.

"Do as I say and be quick about it."

She hastily wriggles out of skirt, panty hose, and blouse. Wearing only her panties, she kneels on the carpet. I pick up the handcuffs and unlock them with their tiny key.

"Hold out your wrists," I say.

"Do you have a tie?" she says.

"What?"

"A silk tie. Do you have one?"

"I don't know," I say. "I guess so. Why?"

"I think it would be really interesting to have you bind my wrists with a silk tie," she says. The thought of it alone is turning her on. Well, what the hell, whatever turns her on.

"Just a minute," I say. "I'll find one."

I creak slowly into the bedroom closet and rummage around. I have worn ties about four times in the past three years, but I still have a couple dozen of them hanging on a rack. The trouble is that there is even less light in the closet than in the bar, and with my shades on I can't see a thing. I'd change to my clear glasses, but I forget where I put them.

I try to pull a bunch of ties off the rack to look at in better light, and the whole thing falls to the floor. Cursing, I pick up the rack and the mess of ties and drag them out into the light. I select one of them—not pure silk but still far too good a tie to be binding up wrists with—and creak back to Edith.

"Is it real silk?" she says.

"No, goddamn it, but it will goddamn well do," I say. "Now hold out your goddamn wrists."

She holds out her wrists and I wrap the tie tightly around them and make a knot.

"Get on your knees and elbows," I say.

She does.

"O.K.," I say, walking around to her upraised tush, "this is for asking if it's real silk. . . ." I give her a hard open-handed smack on the right buttock. "This is for asking for a tie instead of handcuffs," I say, giving her a second smack. "This is for wearing panty hose," I say, giving her a third. "This is for 'I'm sure you're probably right.' " I give her a fourth. "This is for the limes." A fifth. "And this is for the Stolichnaya." A sixth. "This is for requesting vodka when I offered you gin." A seventh. "This is for coming late when you should have been kneeling at my steps at least an hour before you were due." An eighth. "And this is for—"

"Could you switch sides?" she says. "The right one is starting to get numb."

"You're telling me how to *spank* you?" I say, enraged. "You're giving me advice on *technique?*"

"I'm sorry. I just thought—"

"Don't think Don't give me advice on how to punish you I'm right-handed, so I spank on the right!"

I yank at the waistband of her panties and pull them down below her cheeks.

"This is for telling me how to spank you," I say, giving her a ninth smack on her by now quite red flesh.

Just then the phone rings. When I am making love, I never answer the phone. But when I'm spanking?

I pick up the phone.

"What is it?" I say.

"What's wrong with *you?*" says the voice at the other end. It's my next-door neighbor, Fred.

"Nothing," I say. "What's up, Fred?"

"I was wondering if you'd like to go grab a bite to eat," he says.

"I can't right now, I'm busy," I say.

"What're you doing?"

"You wouldn't believe me if I told you," I say.

"Try me."

"I'm spanking someone," I say.

"I don't believe you," he says.

"Suit yourself, Fred. I'll talk to you later," I say and hang up the phone.

"You actually told someone you were spanking me?" says Edith.

"I didn't say it was you I was spanking," I say.

"I can't believe you actually said that on the phone," she says.

"I can't believe how insolent you are," I say. "Who the hell told you to eavesdrop on my telephone conversations?"

"I'm sorry."

"You're not now, but you *will* be," I say and creak over to the bedroom, where I've left the wrist and ankle shackles. I am bathing in sweat inside my leather jacket and pants. I unzip the jacket and throw it onto the floor.

"Come in here," I say. "And don't you dare utter so much as another word."

Edith stands up and walks into the bedroom.

"Lie down on the bed," I growl.

She does. I pull off her panties, attach straps to both her ankles and snap the ends of the chains into the screw eyes. I start to untie the tie from around her wrists and realize it'll be hopeless with my shades on. I take them off and struggle myopically with the knot. I'm sweaty and hot and in a terrible mood. I pull off my boots and my sweaty leather jeans and again attack the knot, but it's still hopeless. I sigh and get a scissors and cut it apart.

"I'm ruining a perfectly good tie because of you," I mutter.

"At least it isn't real silk," she says.

"Did I tell you to talk? Did I? *Did* I?"

"I'm sorry," she says.

I strap her into the wrist shackles and, after lots of adjustments in chain length, manage to snap the ends into the screw eyes in the platform. She is finally spread-eagled on the bed and completely helpless, but it has been a hot and tiring process. Somehow I hadn't expected being a sadist to be such hard work.

"Could I please just say one single thing?" she says.

"What?"

"The straps on my ankles aren't really very tight."

"You'll pay for telling me that," I say and kneel on the floor and adjust her ankle straps.

When I have finished, it occurs to me that I have temporarily run out of sadistic ideas. Oh, I suppose I could simply go on spanking her, but what a bore for both of us. It also occurs to me that I never finished making our drinks. I stand up and go to the bar and mix myself a vodka and tonic and drink it straight down. I make a second one and walk back to the bed.

"Is that one for me?" she says.

"No," I say, "it's for me. I know I never gave you your drink, but if I try to give you this, it'll just dribble down your face and go all over the bed."

"Not if you hold my head and help me," she says.

"Yes it will," I say, but finally I take pity on her and on her ridiculous spread-eagled position and I hold her head and help her drink and it dribbles down her face and goes all over the bed. The funny thing is, though, that I don't really care that much. The funny thing is that I kind of like holding her head. The funny thing is that, even though I'm sure it's strictly against the rules, I feel like kissing her a little, so I do and it's kind of fun and she doesn't seem to mind it, either.

I keep kissing her and stroking her, and we are both beginning to get very turned on.

"You can be very tender when you want to," she whispers.

I sigh a deep sigh.

"Yes, I can," I say.

"You're a funny kind of sadist," she says.

"You're an even funnier kind of masochist," I say. "You're probably the pushiest masochist in New York."

I notice a peculiar expression on her face.

"What is that peculiar expression on your face?" I say.

"I have a confession to make to you," she says.

"What's that?"

"Well, I'm working sort of," she says.

"Working?"

"Yes, I'm researching a book on masochism in women," she says.

"Are you *serious*?" I say, starting to laugh. She says she is, and there is no reason not to believe her. Come to think of it, would a true masochist *demand* Stolichnaya vodka? Still, it's the kind of thing that's only believable in real life and not in fiction.

"Well, *I'm* researching an article for *Playboy*," I say.

We collapse with laughter. It's perfect—not only are the mail-order queens and the hookers I've been in contact with so far on this piece phonies but so is the sole masochist I've managed to flush out of the bushes. And so am I, of course.

"You know what I'd really like to do?" says Edith when she is finally able to speak.

"What would you really like to do?" I say.

"I'd like you to undo these silly chains and then I'd like you to hump my brains out."

"Edith, old buddy," I say, "you've got yourself a deal."

VENGEANCE

FINE VENGEANCE, like fine wine, takes years to ripen.

My tale of revenge begins about twelve years ago. The scene is the elegant Four Seasons Restaurant in Manhattan. I am seated at a table with half a dozen members of New York's snobbish Food Establishment, including the rotund and celebrated gourmet cook and cookbook writer James Beard.

At the time of which I speak the Four Seasons is owned by Restaurant Associates, I am an advertising copywriter, and R.A. is one of my accounts. I have been brought to this noon gathering by the then-President of R.A., Joseph Baum, who is one of the world's great restaurateurs, having created scores of spectacular eateries including Windows on the World, the Forum of the Twelve Caesars, and the Four Seasons itself.

The occasion of this high-powered get-together is that these six haute-cuisine mavens are here to vote on which sauce shall be served with the sole offered on the Four Seasons menu. Grim-faced, tuxedoed captains bring us eight consecutive dishes of the identical sole accompanied by infinitessimally different sauces. All six food snobs take one bite from each dish and make appropriate foodsnobby comments having little meaning to a neophyte like me. Although I have no love for fish, I inhale eight entire servings, being at the time ravenous and poor and willing to ingest any gourmet meal I get for free, regardless of content.

By the end of the eighth dish I am the only one at the table who has not made momentous critical pronouncements on the food. Joe Baum turns to me and asks me my opinion of what I've tasted. I decide I'm not knowledgeable to say anything intelligent and so opt for the role of buffoon: "Well, Joe," I say, flicking ashes off an imaginary Groucho Marx cigar, "I think you've got a helluva restaurant here, but you oughta vary the menu more."

This poignant attempt at humor is greeted with deafening silence. Then, seeing a chance to have a little fun at my expense, James Beard begins to taunt me about my paucity of food knowledge. Space limitations forbid a recitation of all the things he thinks to taunt me about or the level of my innocence. Suffice to say I felt in those days that a *chevre* might just possibly be an automobile. (It's *not* an automobile, it's a goat cheese—you knew that, of course, didn't you?)

I remember thinking to myself, as prickly sweat soaked through my shirt, "Someday I'll get you for this, Beard—I don't know how and I don't know when, but someday, somehow, I'm going to make you pay for what you're doing to me."

We now dissolve to a scene about a year later. I have left advertising to become a freelance writer. Joe Baum and I have gotten to be good friends. I am in the country home of Joe and his wife Ruth for lunch, and around the table is coming a magnum of Chateau Lafite Rothschild 1955 which doubtlessly costs about as much as a tank truck full of Sunoco. As I begin to pour it into my glass, Joe says to me as follows: "Say, Dan, don't you want to pour that with the label up?"

"I don't know, Joe," I say, "why would I want to do a thing like that?"

"Because," he says, "when red wine is resting in the rack the sediment settles to the bottom. If you pour it with the label up, it will be in a position close to the one it was in while in the rack and you'll disturb the sediment as little as possible."

"I see," I say. It doesn't matter that this bottle of wine has been out of the rack awhile, standing upright, and that Joe is doing a bit of a foodsnob number on me himself, because I am certain that the information he has given me will prove invaluable to me in time to come.

We now dissolve to our final scene, about two years later. We are in Joe's city apartment for dinner, on my right is James Beard, whom I haven't seen since my demeaning experience with him at the Four Seasons, and around the table is coming an extraordinary bottle of 1964 Meursault. Beard begins to pour the wine into his glass. Without even thinking what I am doing, I hear the following words walk out of my mouth: "Say, Jim, don't you want to pour that with the label up?"

Beard gets very red in the face, puts the bottle down on the table, turns it around, picks it up and begins to pour it again with the label up. At which point I hear myself saying, "Oh, Jim, you don't *really* have to pour it with the label up—white wine has no *sediment*."

The redness in Beard's face turns a deep purple. Diners on both sides of us suppress gleeful titters. Vengeance, as the Lord Himself often sayeth, is finally mine.

PEOPLE who have been to Haiti are fond of telling people who are about to go there for the first time a lot of things to scare their pants off.

"The minute you get off the plane in Haiti," said a friend of mine with a flair for turgid metaphor, "the sense of evil of the place will envelop you like a warm bath." Another friend said ominously, "Wherever you are in Haiti, day or night, you can always hear the sound of voodoo drums." There are dark hints in a few of the books I've read about Haiti that some of the sacrifices in voodoo are "goats without horns." Humans.

Even your normally jolly travel books get a little glassy-eyed when they tell you about Haiti. "Cats are conspicuously absent from the streets," says the 1975 edition of *Fielding's Guide to the Caribbean*, "and the reason is mildly chilling: the people eat them." And elsewhere in the same book: "Cross a Haitian and you'll regret it: one of the most popular ways of vindicating alienation of affection is for a jilted lady to bite off her rival's lower lip."

Technically, I had been to Haiti once before: I spent an

anxious hour between planes in the Port-au-Prince airport some nine years ago, watched by a huge poster of Papa Doc Duvalier and a sprinkling of soldiers with sunglasses and submachine guns. I remember doing a lot of strained smiling at everybody, keeping my hands out of my pockets in plain view, and being so aware of not making anything that looked like a suspicious sudden movement that I felt as if I was walking under water.

If somebody at the airport nine years ago had told me I'd be coming back to Haiti to go to voodoo ceremonies, I'd have told him to bite his lower lip.

AND YET, on the afternoon of December 30, 1974, here I am again, disembarking from a plane at the Port-au-Prince airport and being enveloped by a sense of evil like a warm bath. Happily, the submachine guns of the Papa Doc era have been replaced by the rather ordinary-looking service revolvers of the Baby Doc era, but as I go through Customs and Immigration I again find myself smiling a bit too much and moving as if underwater.

Peeling off layers of New York sweaters, my friend Dory and I proceed by cab through the hot, sweaty city of Port-au-Prince to the cool stillness of the Ibo Lélé Hotel, up in the mountains. Ibo Lélé happens to be the name of one of the voodoo gods, but the hotel is peaceful and pretty, and as yet we cannot detect the sound of drums, and we see nobody missing a lower lip or eating a cat, so we begin to relax.

We introduce ourselves to Jacques Baussan, a serious, soft-spoken, immaculately dressed, light-skinned Haitian with a very dry sense of humor and a flawless command of English. Baussan was born and raised in Haiti, but for reasons best known to himself went to high school in the Bronx. He is not only the owner of our hotel but a possible voodoo contact.

I tell Baussan of my interest in the occult and he seems

for a while to be indulging me, asking a polite question here, making a noncommittal comment there, and I figure it is useless to ask him anything about voodoo. Then he tells me of a vision he once had while awake, of nineteen men, including seven of his friends, being shot by a Haitian firing squad. Baussan went to all seven of the friends in his vision and begged them to get out of Haiti. All seven pooh–poohed the vision. Two days later, Haitian soldiers rounded up nineteen men, including the seven Baussan had seen in his vision, and a firing squad shot them all to death.

I tell Baussan I am anxious to see voodoo, and that a driver named Eugène César has been recommended to me. Baussan says the first place I should go is something called Le Peristil, that I should see a man there named Monsieur Beauvoir, and that Eugène César is expected here momentarily.

Almost at these very words, a very large, very powerful-looking black man with a mustache and a less than flawless grasp of English appears and is introduced to us as Eugène César. He will be delighted to take us to Le Peristil, he says, and will pick us up in the hotel lobby at nine-thirty. We haven't been in Haiti more than an hour and already I have made two voodoo contacts and we are scheduled to attend our first voodoo ceremony. It all seems effortless.

At nine-forty p.m., Dory and I and a young couple named Larry and Jennifer get into Eugène's car, and we set out for Le Peristil. I had toyed briefly with the idea of renting a car and doing my own driving but am soon thankful that Eugène is doing the work instead. The mountain roads are narrow and winding and steep and unlit, and even with Eugène's experienced handling we have several near collisions before arriving at Le Peristil, at the edge of the water.

Le Peristil is a sort of combination open-air nightclub and voodoo temple. There is an audience of fifty or sixty people, partly tourist and partly Haitian, sitting facing a slightly raised concrete platform upon which the ceremonies have already begun. Above the platform is a thatched conical roof. On the platform are about thirty people—three drummers; a voodoo priest, or *houngan*; a voodoo priestess, or *mambo*; and a number of dancers.

The dancers are mostly women and wear short skirts and brief blouses with exposed midriffs. The drummers are drumming with great gusto, and everybody is dancing and chanting and passing around a large sequined bottle of cheap rum called *clairin* and then spitting it out in huge, vaporous clouds. I drift closer to the stage for a better view of what is going on.

What is going on just now is that one of the dancing women has been given two large white pigeons, and holding them by the legs, she is waving them around over her head, dancing in increasingly wilder gyrations, taking more and mores swigs of *clairin* from the sequined bottle, and generally carrying on in a crazy-assed manner.

I have read enough about voodoo to know that the rhythms of the drums are supposedly capable of inducing altered states of consciousness in the drummers themselves, and I know that the object of voodoo ceremonies is for the participants to become possessed by their gods and that sacrifices of birds and animals are involved. But as I watch the woman with the pigeons begin an erratic series of convulsive jerks, I am scarcely prepared for what happens next.

Suddenly the woman is holding only one of the pigeons and ripping the feathers out of its wings, and suddenly she has opened her mouth and bitten the pigeon's head off with an audible crunch, and then she has swallowed it.

I stand there aghast, slightly nauseous, staring in amazed disbelief at the possessed woman now holding the headless white body aloft, now drinking blood from its neck. Well, I think, this is what you have come to Haiti to see, and now you have seen it, and I hope you are satisfied. A sudden commotion off to my right distracts me and I rush to see what has happened, thankful to get away from headless pigeons for a moment.

Two dozen members of the audience are crowded around a makeshift railing above the sea. I peer into the dark waters and see three people thrashing about: the priest and priestess and the lady who's just bitten the pigeon's head off. The priest is brandishing a very large sword, and I have a sudden fantasy that he is a distant cousin of the pigeon and we are about to see a little of that well-known Haitian vengeance.

A tall, extremely handsome Haitian materializes at my side, and I ask him what is going on. He replies in perfect English that the lady who's chowed down the pigeon has done so to strengthen the power of the goddess of the sea, who'd possessed her and who'd then compelled her to rush into the water. Voodoo sacrifices are made to specific gods and goddesses, to revitalize them. In gratitude, these revitalized spirits temporarily occupy the sacrificer's body and give them power to do a number of peppy but tasteless things.

I ask what swell things are going to happen next, and he says more possessions and some purifications by fire. We talk further, and then it strikes me who he is. "You are Monsieur Beauvoir, aren't you?" I say.

He owns up to being Beauvoir, and I tell him that I've been given his name by my new best friend, Jacques Baussan. I tell him of my interest in the occult and that I am writing a book about it, and I say that I have even discovered some psychic powers in myself. Many people in my country, I say, are turning to the occult, perhaps because they have lost faith in their political leaders and in God and are seeking something else to believe in.

Although I believe this last thing to be more or less true, I have mainly said it to see what effect it will have on Beauvoir. It seems to have a good effect, because the next thing that Beauvoir says to me is this: "Would you like to take part in the ceremony tonight?"

"Uh, sure," I say. "I mean, doing what, for example?"

"Saluting the goddess who will possess one of the women at the end," he says.

"Uh, by doing what, though?" I say.

"I will let you know," says Beauvoir. "When the time comes."

The priest and priestess have by now dragged the pigeon biter out of the water and resumed the ceremony. Beauvoir tells me to cross in front of the concrete platform and sort of hunker down and wait for further instructions. I start off in the direction he has indicated, and when I reach the front of the platform, I step into a space between the stage and the audience area and my boot becomes inextricably wedged there.

The more I try to pull my boot out of the space the more the space doesn't want it to leave. So there I stand, with wild voodoo things taking place on my right and people who are having trouble seeing past me on my left, and finally there is nothing to do but take my foot out of my boot and hop out of everybody's way.

A short time later, Beauvoir ambles by, spots my forlorn boot sticking up into the air, and rips it out of its prison, neatly sacrificing about an inch and a half of heel in the process. He hands back the boot and tells me to wait for his signal.

I wait. I do not know what I am waiting for exactly. I know that saluting a possessed woman probably entails more than whipping my right hand smartly to my brow. I figure that whatever it is it will be good for the book. Bad for me, good for the book.

Meanwhile, on stage a second woman is getting possessed. She is taking many swigs out of the bottle of *clairin* and belching out huge clouds of vapor, dancing more and more wildly, and slipping into a few fast convulsions. Kerosene is poured on the concrete stage and lit. As the flames whoosh upward, the possessed woman dances barefoot into them for a longish time, at length collapses, and is carried off by a couple of dancers.

Now it's a gentleman's turn. He also takes huge gulps of *clairin* and spews them out in a cloud, dances more and more wildly, and does a convulsion or two. I watch to see if he will toast his tootsies or bite a bird, and as I am watching, he starts rubbing an empty drinking glass sensuously over his body. Without warning, he bites down savagely on the glass. I am close enough to hear the shattering of the glass and the crunching of the pieces as he chews them up and swallows them. When he is not more than halfway through his snack he collapses and is carried off by the dancers.

The next soloist—the whole process has begun to remind me of jazz musicians standing up and doing a little riff and then sitting down to great applause—is another woman. Her specialty is that, upon becoming possessed, she shinnies up the center pole to the thatched roof some fifteen feet in the air and thrashes about like a drunken monkey. She hangs by one arm, she hangs by one leg, she hangs upside down, and her left boob accidentally pops out of her bodice, but still it is not what I would call one of your flashier possessions.

At length, she shinnies back down the pole, flings herself around the stage, and falls off it onto a startled tourist holding a Rolleiflex and a strobe unit. She collapses on him, boob and all, and then the dancers come and carry her off to her dressing room.

More kerosene is poured on the stage and lit, but before anyone else can get possessed it goes out. Still more kerosene is poured and lit. A very tiny lady gets possessed and shuffles into the fire for a neat time-step. Then she picks up some smoldering pieces of wood that have been lying in the fire and chews them up and swallows them. I am toying with a theory of how voodoo gods seem to have an oral fixation when I spot Beauvoir walking slowly up onto the stage. He then turns and looks in my direction and gives me the high sign.

Well, I think, here we go. I get up and walk uncertainly onto the stage. My heart is ramming away pretty good inside my chest. Behind me I can feel dozens of audience members silently wondering what the hell a white guy in a safari jacket and boots of different heel heights is doing in a Haitian voodoo ceremony.

I lean toward Beauvoir's ear and ask him in a whisper what I'm supposed to do.

"Watch what *I* do," he whispers. "Then, when I'm finished, you do the same."

Beauvoir approaches the possessed lady, who is finishing off the last few bites of smoldering sticks. She extends her right arm to him, bent at the elbow. He extends his right elbow to her. They touch right elbows. Then she extends her left elbow and they touch left elbows. Then they link right arms and do a step I seem to remember from square dancing. Then they link left arms and do a little number in the opposite direction, squatting till they touch the floor and then bobbing back up again.

So far so good, I think. Nothing that a Jewish kid from Illinois with a little square-dance background couldn't handle.

Then the tiny possessed woman grasps Beauvoir around the waist—he outweighs her by an easy one hundred and fifty pounds—and hoists him up into the air and carries him around the stage. She puts him down, then picks up some smoldering coals, takes each of his hands, and rubs the coals across his palms.

Greenburg, I think, you are in terrible trouble. You have been warned about situations like this—about being invited to do things with fire that would not harm a black Haitian voodoo person at all, but that would do severe damage to a white person of Hebraic descent, and now you are really in trouble, because either you will refuse to do it and offend delicate feelings of vengeful Haitians or their gods, or else you will go along with it and never be able to play patty-cakes again.

The lady has finished with Beauvoir and turns to me.

"Now, it is *your* turn," says Beauvoir to me needlessly.

Oh, God, I think, please tell me what I should do here. Please tell me which is better, charred palms or deeply offended, vengeful Haitians.

The lady extends her right arm to me, bent at the elbow. Not knowing what else to do, I extend mine and we touch. She extends her left elbow and I extend mine and we touch again. She extends her right arm, we link and do a fast step in a clockwise direction. I still don't know what I am going to do. So far, I seem to be going along with it, is what I seem to be doing.

We link left arms and do a few steps in the opposite direction. Maybe, I think, it will not be a disgusting, disfiguring third-degree burn at all. Maybe it will be only an innocuous little flush of warmth that is curable by ice cubes and Solarcaine. We do more dance steps and lots of bobbing up and down. Then she extends the littlest finger of her right hand to me. What is this, ad-libbing? I extend the littlest finger of *my* right hand and we link pinkies. The last time I did this was when we made bets in grammar school. Maybe the lady has just bet me I will bolt for the sea when she hands me the hot coals.

Suddenly she grabs me around the waist and hoists me into the air. She starts walking around the stage with me, but somehow her grip isn't tight enough and I slide out of her arms to the floor. Seemingly enraged, she shoots one arm between my legs, throws the other arm around my waist, and lifts me roofward in a sort of modified firemen's crotch-carry. She walks around the stage with me like this for awhile, and it is such an uncomfortable position in which to be carried that I have temporarily forgotten about the coals, and maybe so has she, because suddenly it is all over. The woman has collapsed and been carried offstage and I have never had to find out what I would have done with the hot coals.

I hobble offstage, my gait influenced by recent groin pressure and by one heel being impressively shorter than the other, and I locate Beauvoir, whose palms appear to be in mint condition. I ask Beauvoir if it's a usual thing for a tourist to get to participate in a voodoo ceremony and he says no, it's a special honor. I am feeling very elated and excited and, mainly, very relieved about the whole affair, but there is still one thing which is puzzling me.

"Listen," I say to Beauvoir, "you weren't in a trance when you were up there, right?"

"No," says Beauvoir.

"Then, how come the coals didn't burn your hands?"

"Because," he says, "the power of the gods protected me."

"I see," I say. The power of the gods, eh? So *that's* how they do it.

"If you had handled the coals," says Beauvoir, "the gods would have protected you as well."

Fat chance.

To CELEBRATE my deliverance, Dory and Eugène and I drive to a nearby discotheque for a drink. Twice we are overcharged, for admission tickets and drinks. Twice Eugène raises a big stink and gets our money refunded. I put my arm around Eugène and tell him he is some terrific guy, and I buy him a lot of rum punches. We all get fairly looped.

Somehow we make it back to the hotel. Before we go inside, Eugène asks to speak to me in private. I say sure.

"You like to see de real voodoo witch doctor?" he says.

"As opposed to what?" I say. "I mean, what was it we saw tonight, chopped liver?"

Eugène looks blank.

"Weren't the guys at Le Peristil tonight real?" I say.

Eugène shrugs.

"Tonight ees for tourists," says Eugène. "Thees doctor I know, he ees not for tourists. He make de real voodoo. He can also teach you to do de voodoo for yourself."

Hmmmm. I am upset to hear Eugène imply that what I thought was a real voodoo ceremony was primarily for tourists. I could have gotten third-degree burns, and they wouldn't even have been authentic. I will later learn that the voodoo at Le Peristil was authentic enough, but for now I am intrigued by the idea of a private audience with a real witch doctor, particularly one who can teach me how to do voodoo myself.

"When did you want me to meet this man?" I say.

"Tomorrow night," says Eugène.

Tomorrow night. New Year's Eve. I *had* had my heart set on getting hold of a short-wave radio and waltzing till the wee hours to the music of Guy Lombardo. But how many chances do you get to learn voodoo from a real witch doctor?

"Are Larry and Jennifer invited?" I say.

"Oh no," says Eugène, clearly appalled at such a thought, "thees ees for *real* voodoo. Not for tourists."

Somehow, perhaps because I have taken part in a voodoo ceremony for tourists, Eugène no longer considers me a tourist.

"O.K.," I say, "let's do it. What time shall I meet you?"

"I peek you up nine-thirty een de lobby," says Eugène.

PROMPTLY at nine-thirty the following night, Dory and I get into Eugène's car, and we set out to find the real witch doctor. In the car is a Haitian friend of Eugène's, who is not introduced. I figure there is a reason for this having to do with real witch doctors, and I don't introduce myself either.

We drive down the mountain and then for a seemingly interminable time on flat ground into the boondocks. We pass through a military checkpoint and Eugène babbles in Creole to the soldiers, who look in at us, babble some more, then let us through. We stop several times to ask directions of various natives in the dark. Finally we pull up outside a large concrete shed, and Eugène motions for us to get out. We do.

Eugène and his unintroduced friend lead us into the concrete shed, where we are presented to the real witch doctor. The real witch doctor is a very black Haitian, between the ages of forty and sixty-five, who wears horn-rimmed glasses, a short-sleeved print sport shirt, and a silver bracelet with what appears to be a Masonic emblem on it. He speaks no English, so whatever he or Dory or I say is translated by either Eugène or his friend or, in most cases, both.

The real witch doctor shows us around the concrete shed, which, it develops, is a real voodoo temple. Then the real witch doctor opens each of three tiny locked storage rooms and shows us hundreds of real voodoo artifacts. How you tell real voodoo artifacts from fake voodoo artifacts is that the fake ones look real and the real ones look fake.

For example, the way you know that this witch doctor is real is that no fake witch doctor would dare to have things like a miniature white rubber skull with a black Dynel wig sitting atop an empty Johnny Walker Red Label bottle on his desk. And no fake witch doctor would have the hotel desk clerk's bell and the two Frosty-the-Snowman Christmas cards and the two American one-dollar bills and the one Haitian dollar bill under the clear plastic slipcover that is also on his desk. And no fake witch doctor would have, among the bottles he uses for real voodoo purposes, an empty bottle labeled Manischewitz Concord Grape Wine either, but this one does.

Eugène can't seem to get over how real everything is here tonight and how fake everything was at Le Peristil last night, and he keeps dropping remarks to this effect every thirty seconds.

The real witch doctor asks through his interpreters whether we would like our cards read. We say sure. He sits down at his desk, beneath a sputtering fluorescent light that will not last the night, and takes out a pack of what once must have been playing cards. It is impossible to tell what they are now, because they are so cracked and falling to pieces. The cards are brownish and rather thick and rather old and rather grotesque looking, and if somebody had confided to me that they were made of human skin, I would not have doubted it for an instant. The fronts of the cards are indistinguishable from the backs, except that afterward Dory tells me she thinks she can make out that one of the cards is the joker.

The real witch doctor takes out a large bottle of cheap rum wrapped in red-and-black cloth, and a pitcher of water and a candle. He lights the candle and passes it to Dory. He tells her through Eugène that she must concentrate on the questions she would like answered while she holds the candle. Then she is to take the pitcher of water, step outside, and pour a few drops on the ground two times. Then she is to sit down and cut the cards three times. She manages all these tasks with startling ease.

Next the real witch doctor hits his desk-clerk bell and passes the pack of cards over the flames several times. He lays the cards out in front of him, a row at a time, uttering phrases in Creole as each row is laid out. Eugène and his friend provide simultaneous translations.

After Dory's cards are read I go through the same process. I believe it would be a violation of Dory's privacy to tell you here what the witch doctor said about her cards, but I will gladly tell you about mine because, first of all, I have already stated lots of private things about myself in print before and because, second, although you may have had somebody read your cards at some point in your life, you have probably never had them read by a real witch doctor in Haiti and I insist on giving you the feeling of what such an experience is like.

Here, then, are the translations by Eugène and his friend of what the real witch doctor learns about me from reading my cards, and to hell with privacy.

After the first row of cards: "Weetch doctor he say a mon ees your friend, and you make sometheeng for heem, and now that mon ees no more your friend."

"Mmmmm," I reply, careful not to reveal too much.

After the second row of cards: "Weetch doctor he say once you are seeck een bed, een hospeetol, and eef de spirit of a certain woman not protect you, then you die."

After the third row of cards: "Weetch doctor he say sometimes you are weak, and then sometimes you are strong."

Holy Ned, I think to myself, the bastard has really got me now. Next thing you know he'll break out in a chorus of "Sometimes you're happy, sometimes you're blu-ue. . . ."

After the fourth row of cards: "Weetch doctor he say he see you make a lot of money very easy, very soon."

I believe what we have here is an instance of what is really a rather common phenomenon in the occult world, that of the card reader accidentally mistaking his client's fortune for that of his own. I don't believe I can take much more of this, not in front of all these people. It's far too personal.

"Weetch doctor he say de reading ees over," says Eugène's friend. "He say you owe heem twenty dollar."

I figure twenty is a little steep, but I generally make it a practice not to haggle fees with either psychiatrists or holy men, and besides the first three beauties he gave me *alone* are easily worth $6.66 apiece. I cough up the double sawbuck and hand it over to the real witch doctor, who says something else in Creole.

"Weetch doctor he say maybe you like other theengs," says Eugène's friend.

"Like what?" I say.

The real witch doctor says something in Creole.

"He say maybe you like to stay here four or five nights, sleep on floor, learn real voodoo."

I look at the floor and try to envision myself sleeping on it for four or five nights.

"Tell the doctor, no thanks," I say. "Maybe some other time."

The witch doctor says something else.

"He say maybe you like to make some black magic," says Eugène's friend.

My ears perk up.

"Like what?" I say.

The witch doctor says something else.

"He say maybe you like to take a dagger, steeck heem eento a melon, cause somebody to die," says Eugène's friend.

"Tell the doctor, no thanks on that too," I say.

The witch doctor says something else, at fairly greater length. Eugène translates this for me.

"He say because you come to see heem and hov your cards read, so he geev you special voodoo blesseeng on any silver chain you hove weeth you. Also make very strong voodoo lotion to rub on body and prepare voodoo potion to dreenk and voodoo prayer card for each one of you."

This seems like a harmless and good-natured package of things, so Dory and I each take off the silver chains we are wearing and hand them to the real witch doctor.

"He say either you can peeck them up een two or three days," says Eugène's friend, "or else he make them appear mogically een your hotel room."

"Is there a charge for all of this?" I say.

Eugène and the witch doctor confer.

"He say four hondred dollar," says Eugène.

I feel the skin on my face become engorged with blood.

"Excuse me," I say, "what was that price again?"

"Four hondred dollar," says Eugène.

I reach across the desk of the witch doctor and take back our two silver chains. The witch doctor says something else.

"He say de price not eemportant to heem," says Eugène. "De doctor weel do thees theengs for you and then you pay heem whatever you can afford to pay heem, even a few pennies."

"I'm afraid not," I say, motioning to Dory to stand up.

The witch doctor says something else.

"He say he do eet for you for two hondred dollar, and you can geev heem part of eet now and de rest when you get home," says Eugène.

"I don't think we are interested in what the doctor has to offer at any price at all," I say and start edging toward the door.

The witch doctor says something else.

"He say one hondred dollar he can do eet for, but dat ees de lowest he can do eet," says Eugène's friend.

I extend my hand to the witch doctor, grasp his firmly, and look deep into his eyes.

"Good-bye, doctor," I say. "I really mean that."

I lead Dory, Eugène, and his friend back to the car, and we silently get inside and start up and turn around and head back toward the hotel. I am so angry I can barely speak.

How is it that Eugène, who is a friend of a friend of a friend of mine in New York, who prevented us so heroically from getting ripped off at the discotheque last night, could set us up for a four-hundred-dollar rip-off the very next night? How could I have been so stupid as to trust anybody in such circumstances in any case?

Well, I figure, on the one hand, here we are in a very strange and violent land where people eat cats and bite other people's lips off, and we are also the only white folks within miles. And on the other hand, I have been taught in therapy to get my feelings out and there are some very definite feelings I would like to get out now, no matter what the consequences.

Perhaps there is even a way for me to say it and still keep all parts of my body intact.

"Eugène," I say at last, "I am very sad."

"Why?" says Eugène after a little while.

"I think you know," I say. No reply seems to be forthcoming from Eugène, so I continue. "We have been in Haiti now only two days, Eugène, but everybody has been so wonderful to us, and we have been having such a good time, and now tonight it is spoiled. I think sometimes that I am too trusting. Too naïve. You know the word naïve, Eugène?"

"Yes," says Eugène.

"I think I am too naïve, Eugène," I say. "I think that I see somebody I like and I am too willing to trust him and that is not such a good thing. And you know what else I think, Eugène?"

"What?" says Eugène.

"I know that Americans are very rich and Haitians are very poor and that it is a great temptation to take from the rich and give to the poor, but I think there is also something that is just as important, and that is respect between people. And communication. And friendship. And trust."

Eugène says nothing. Eugène's friend says nothing. They don't seem to be very proud of themselves. Real voodoo is very strong, but stronger yet is Jewish guilt.

I look at my watch. It is precisely twelve midnight.

"Happy goddamned New Year," I say.

THE BEST-KNOWN hotel in Haiti is the Oloffson. Graham Greene's novel *The Comedians* was set there, the film of the same name was shot there, and every famous person who comes to Haiti seems to stay there. Its owner, Al Seitz, is allegedly the model for the character that Richard Burton played in the movie version of *The Comedians*. Al Seitz also happens to be one of my contacts for real voodoo. Dory and I decide to pay Al Seitz a visit.

Having given up Eugène, I haggle cab fares with another driver at the hotel, and soon Dory and I are riding down the mountain into town. On our way we almost have a head-on collision with a motorcade that is coming fast in the other direction.

With sirens screaming and red lights flashing, our cab is rocked by the wash of about half a dozen motorcycles, followed by several police cars and a good half dozen Mercedes-Benzes packed with military brass and soldiers with gun barrels pointed out the windows. From one of the Mercedes-Benzes we catch an almost subliminal glimpse of President Baby Doc Duvalier throwing fistfuls of money out the window to his people. And then they are gone.

Haitian architecture is an appealing hodgepodge of extreme out-of-date styles that *Fielding's Guide* thinks was caused by Haitians who visited the 1900 Colonial Fair in Paris: "Presumably they copied the main features from the exhibits they most admired—Chinese pagodas, Indian mosques, Victorian gingerbread. . . ." Well, the Oloffson Hotel is mostly Victorian gingerbread, and it's choked with tropical vegetation and filled with white rattan furniture and palm trees and enormous ceiling fans and you sort of expect at any moment to stumble over Sidney Greenstreet in a white suit. It is hard to imagine a more ideal setting for a Graham Greene story.

Dory and I go into the Oloffson bar and sit down and immediately spot what we are looking for: holding forth on all subjects having to do with Haiti to an audience of four tourists is a huge, fat, gray-haired fellow with an American accent. It is clearly Al Seitz.

When he gets up and comes to the bar for a refill, I say to him as follows: "Mr. Seitz, my name is Dan Greenburg, I'm a writer from New York, and I'd like to buy you a drink."

He looks at me bemusedly and replies: "Well, I'm not Al Seitz, I'm Major Bob Cunningham, retired, formerly of the

Canadian Navy, and don't buy me any drinks till you find out if you like me, because I'm a son-of-a-bitch."

We are initially taken with the son-of-a-bitch's outrageous charm and sit down to join his entourage. He introduces us to his party, keeps forgetting our names, and then decides that I'm a dead ringer for Sammy Davis, Jr., and that Dory is one for Barbra Streisand and starts referring to us as Sammy and Barbra, which he finds immensely amusing and which, after the first four dozen references, not many of the rest of us do.

I am wearying of the party and go looking for the real Al Seitz in the Oloffson office. But Seitz is gone, he isn't expected back today, and although I have had enough of Cunningham, when he suggests we all go and see his wife's shop, Dory seems interested, and I figure maybe the wife will have some voodoo contacts, so I agree to go.

Cunningham's wife, Anna, is a plump Haitian lady with great warmth, great sensitivity, a slim working knowledge of English, and an overall human value roughly two dozen times her spouse's.

We buy several carved wooden pieces from Anna, who grants us amazing discounts: "I give you de foctory price," she keeps repeating. We have an amiable conversation until I bring the topic around to voodoo, whereupon she becomes almost violent.

"De weetch doctors, dey try to *fooleesh* de peoples," she says. "Dey fooleesh de peoples just for de money." (Well, *we* certainly don't know any witch doctors who fooleesh people for money.) "I hate de voodoo," says Anna. "I hate what dey doing to de onimals. I make myself and every person een my fomily vegetarian for what dey do to de onimals een de voodoo."

Dory and I, both animal lovers, are very moved. In the background, Cunningham is drinking and yelling obscenities at his son-in-law. It seems that Cunningham asked his son-in-law to drive us home and offered him money to do it, where-upon the son-in-law refused.

"No first-closs peoples een Haiti take money for to do peo-ples favors," Anna explains, and she offers to drive us herself. We protest; she insists.

When Anna drops us off we have a very emotional farewell.

"I hope you write dot de peoples should not to hurt de onimals for de voodoo," she says to me, "and not to always be so crazy for making de money. De peoples should theenk very poseeteev, be strong, hov respect for de privacy of them-self and de other peoples, and remember that we all de same and we all hov to die sometimes, even eef you a president or a weetch doctor or a preence. I don't write thees myself be-cause myself I om, how you say, eel—eeleet—"

"Illiterate?" I say.

She nods and we all say goodbye again.

DESPITE my feelings about animals, I have come to Haiti to see the real voodoo, and I am going to see the real voodoo if it kills me.

It is the following morning and I am on the phone at the Ibo Lélé, running down voodoo contacts for about two hours straight, with not one completed phone call to show for my efforts. On many of my calls the switchboard is busy and I have to wait for a line. When I get a line, the operator for-gets the number and has to ask me again, or dials it wrong, or both. Almost every number I call is first busy, then out of order, then busy again, then nobody answers. On the one call I finally manage to get through, technical difficulties develop in mid-conversation and the line goes dead twice.

"As bad as the phones are here," a Haitian confides to me, "they are still better than the mails."

The Ibo Lélé has two slot machines in its recreation room which I play between calls. On the whole, I hit on the slot machines with rather better results than the phones.

That evening, having come up with nothing authentic, we go to another tourist-oriented voodoo ceremony. What this one lacks in authenticity it makes up for in aesthetics. It is run by a Haitian dancer named Katherine Dunham, and the costumes and drumming and dancing are all superb. There are maybe thirty dancers on stage and fewer than that number of people in the audience. There are a few staged possessions, a little walking on fire and handling of live coals and lifting and carrying around of heavy people. Toward the conclusion of the ceremony, a cute little black goat with lighted candles tied to his horns is led out and picked up and carried around by the dancers, and a wicked-looking sword is raised above his head. Mercifully, the goat is not killed.

The following morning, we stop at something called The Perfume Factory to talk to Al Seitz, who owns this as well as the Oloffson Hotel and a number of other outfits. Seitz is white-haired, mod-dressed, Jewish, smart, sassy, charming, helpful, and has an attention span of about sixteen seconds tops. I tell him about our experience with the witch doctor and he chuckles.

"You got off easy," he says.

"How do you mean?" I say.

"The guy you describe," says Seitz, "is a guy called Voodoo Joe, and he happens to be the biggest rip-off artist in all of Haiti.

"Couple of years ago, two ladies I know who are into the occult like yourself decided to take Voodoo Joe up on the offer to stay in his temple and learn voodoo. He charged them thirty or forty bucks a day to sleep on two straw mats on his floor. After a couple of days these gals realize they know more about voodoo than Voodoo Joe and they've been ripped off. They sneak out of there, taking with them the young boy that Voodoo Joe is using as an acolyte and with whom he is apparently having some kind of romance.

"The gals bring this kid back to the Oloffson, check into

one of the rooms, and begin performing voodoo ceremonies. Voodoo Joe appears in my office and demands the return of his acolyte. I just laughed in his face and told him to beat it, so he threatened to put a voodoo curse on me. I said, go ahead. I'm still here, you notice.

"Another time, two guys I know from Europe, Scandinavian dignitaries, went to see Voodoo Joe. He showed them all his voodoo artifacts in the storerooms behind the temple, just like he showed you. Then, when they didn't want to buy anything, he said they owed him a hundred bucks.

"Well, naturally they refused to give it to him. So Voodoo Joe locks them all inside a storeroom, takes out a whip and starts flicking it around the room and demanding the hundred bucks. They still refuse, so he lunges at the smaller of the two guys and tries to strangle him. The other guy manages to get the door unlocked and they beat it out of there and somehow get to the police. By the time they arrive at the police station and call me, there are still finger marks on the smaller guy's neck where Voodoo Joe tried to strangle him. I saw them with my own eyes."

Seitz is right. We did get off easy.

THAT NIGHT, we are invited to cocktails at the home of Harry and Mary Lou Hughes. Harry works for the USIA, and the family has been in Haiti a couple of years now. At the Hughes' is an American professor named Feldman, who tells me about an authentic ceremony he attended while living here.

"Authentic voodoo ceremonies," says Feldman, "are interminable. They go on for hours, sometimes days. You really have to be willing to sit through a lot of boring things before they go to the good stuff."

"Good stuff like what?" I say.

"I've seen possessions," says Feldman, "where the natives involved displayed unbelievable physical strength, where they spoke in strange languages they couldn't possibly have known, where the men spoke in women's voices, the women in men's voices, and a lot of other things like that which don't sound like much when you describe them but which looked very impressive at the time."

Also present at the Hughes' is a Haitian art dealer named Pierre. Most Haitians are either primitive artists or dealers in primitive art. The painters are usually voodoo practitioners—Haitians are 90 percent Catholic and 100 percent voodooist, according to a local saying—so most dealers are excellent contacts for authentic voodoo ceremonies. Pierre vows to get me to an authentic voodoo ceremony before we leave Haiti the day after tomorrow.

In fact, Pierre has been invited to some ceremony or other tonight, but can't remember either where or by whom. He will call tomorrow and give me directions to one he thinks will come off tomorrow night.

The next day, Pierre delivers on his promise and, at my request, dictates elaborate driving directions in French to the desk clerk for me to give whatever driver I end up using.

It is our last night in Haiti. The real voodoo ceremony is to begin about seven and go on most of the night. Dory is not the slightest bit interested in seeing any more sacrifices so I am to go alone. At six-fifteen I kiss her goodbye and go out in front of the hotel to find a driver. The prospect of going alone to a real voodoo ceremony is making me plenty nervous.

There are no drivers in front of the hotel and I am about to do a little light panicking when I spot my old buddy Eugène. Wonderful old Eugène, who set me up for the Four Hundred Dollar Misunderstanding. How could I ever trust Eugène again? On the other hand, at least I have made my feelings known to him, and what guarantee do I have that another driver wouldn't try to rip me off even worse than Eugène?

I walk over to Eugène, give him a wry smile, and say I'd

like to talk. He nods. I tell him I need a driver for the evening, that I have directions to a real voodoo ceremony, and that I am willing to forget about Voodoo Joe if he promises to take better care of me than last time. He nods. We shake hands.

I give Eugène Pierre's directions. He reads them. He says he doesn't understand them. We go back to the desk and the clerk who took down the directions from Pierre and they get into a long discussion in Creole about it. Eugène says he still doesn't know where the place is. I say let's call Pierre and he can explain it to Eugène directly.

I call Pierre, the phone works, and Pierre is in. So far, so good. I tell Pierre that Eugène doesn't know where the place is. Pierre says it's not hard to find, and we are to look for a witch doctor named Silpha; our contact is a one-armed man named Tiboute. I put Eugène on the phone. A fifteen-minute discussion in French ensues. I get back on the phone and ask what the problem is.

"Eugène says he does not know thees place," says Pierre.

"How is that possible?" I say.

"The place where the voodoo ees being done ees een a very bad section of town," says Pierre. "The government forbids drivers to take tourists there. Eugène is afraid to get into trouble. You understand?"

"I understand," I say. "Thank you."

"Please do not tell Eugène I told you thees," says Pierre.

"Don't worry," I say.

I hang up the phone and try to figure out how I am going to talk Eugène into driving me to a voodoo ceremony without acknowledging the fact that I know he doesn't wish to take me.

"Come on, Eugène," I say, "let's give it a try."

"I do not know where ees thees place," says Eugène.

"Come on," I say. "We have the directions. We'll figure them out together."

I lead Eugène to his car and get inside. He gets in the car

very slowly. I ask to see the directions. He doesn't have them.
Neither do I. I go back to the desk clerk and ask for the directions. The desk clerk, whose English has been impeccable
so far, suddenly has great trouble understanding me. I persist
and he finally takes pity on me and slowly, very slowly, hands
over the directions.

I go back and get into the car with Eugène. I feel that the
first step is to get the car in motion. I say that Pierre has ad-
vised me to bring the witch doctor a bottle of rum as a gift.
I ask Eugène to take me to a liquor store.

Eugène puts the car in gear very, very slowly, and we go
down the mountain an inch at a time. Eugène says he has to
deliver a message to someone and stops three times before we
even get to the liquor store.

After a stop for rum and an unexplained change of cars,
we finally set off for the voodoo ceremony.

When we get to the right neighborhood, I see why the government doesn't want tourists to come here. The area is so
awful and depressed-looking it seems unreal—a set for *Porgy
and Bess*, Catfish Row, rather than a place that human beings
actually live in. The unpaved streets are deeply rutted and
treacherous, the houses little more than closets made of planks
or reed mats or corrugated tin all crammed together. Hundreds of people stand about in the streets, looking in on us,
no doubt wondering what a white man is doing in these parts.

I am a little nervous, but I somehow feel that Eugène is
looking out for me. We stop several times for Eugène to ask
directions, and finally he has a couple of little kids get in the
car to direct us to the home of the one-armed man. After a
few stops, we seem to be there. Eugène parks and reparks the
car and takes elaborate precautions locking it up. Then, with
a reassuring smile at me, he leads me through a throng of
people clustered around a smallish concrete building with a
corrugated tin roof.

The building is one room, roughly twenty feet square. The

concrete walls are painted a shade of magenta and a shade of turquoise that have been selected by someone who is either color-blind or has a cosmic sense of humor about color.

Standing against the walls or seated on chairs and benches are about one hundred and forty people. It is impossible to see how one more person can squeeze into the room. It is also impossible to see why I have worn a sweater and a safari jacket, because it is somewhere in the vicinity of 120 degrees in here and climbing.

The drums have started, but the witch doctor has not yet arrived. Every eye in the place is searching me. Some of these people, I feel sure, have never seen a white in the flesh.

Eugène asks for the one-armed man and for Silpha but gets nowhere. He explains that I am a friend of Pierre's, who is a friend of the one-armed man's, who is a friend of Silpha's, and so on. And then a very perky-looking slim person dressed not unlike Sportin' Life in *Porgy and Bess* squeezes into the room, and there is no doubt in my mind that this is Silpha, the *real* real witch doctor.

How I know this is Silpha is (1) that he moves with the authority of a born leader and (2) that he is dressed in just what you would wear to an authentic voodoo ceremony if you were an authentic witch doctor—a turquoise-and-white houndstooth-check short-sleeved safari-style leisure suit with brass buttons.

Eugène and I make our way over to the witch doctor. I explain in broken French that I am a friend of Pierre's, who is a friend of the one-armed man's, and so on. I say I am very honored to meet the witch doctor and to be here in general, and I give him the bottle of rum. The witch doctor raises his hand and two folding chairs are passed over our heads and squeezed down in the front for Eugène and me to sit on.

It is hard to see how there will be room for any voodoo to take place here. There is no raised platform, only a peristyle about a foot square, with a center post running up to the ceiling. As the drumming continues, several women carrying sequined voodoo flags and swords start to dance around the peristyle, and since my knees are about a foot from the peristyle, there are continuous collisions between Jewish and voodoo legs.

The dancing and the drumming continue awhile. Then the witch doctor hops onto the peristyle and, holding on to the center post, signals for the drums to stop. He then points to me and tells me to stand up. Well, I think, awash in my own sweat, here we go again.

The witch doctor motions me to make my way through the press of bodies to the altar, which is under a canopy of blue quilted satin with a red rose pattern. As I reach the altar, a fat, grandmotherly type grabs my arm and hugs me against her body, imprisoning my arm in a warm, viselike grip. She smiles winningly at me, and I return what I hope is something attractive in a facial expression.

The lady is holding a voodoo doll. She takes a second voodoo doll off the altar and offers it to me, saying something in French or Creole.

"What?" I say, *"Je ne comprends pas."*

"You want?" she says, smiling crookedly.

For some idiot reason, it suddenly strikes me that the lady is asking if I want to buy the voodoo doll. That would be my nightmare—haggling over the price of a voodoo doll in the middle of a crowded voodoo temple. I am so mortified that all I can do is repeat the phrase "You want? You want?" as if I didn't understand it.

At length the lady dismisses me as a mental defective and gives the voodoo doll to someone else. Then I get it: it's an honor to stand at the altar during the ceremony and hold the various artifacts. By the time the lady, who still has my arm imprisoned against her, offers me a sequined bottle to hold, I simply accept it without bothering to haggle over price.

I peer about at the other voodoo artifacts being held and

discover that, just as at Voodoo Joe's, the hokier they look, the more authentic they are. The matronly woman on my other side is cradling what must be a very authentic voodoo artifact indeed—a Negro Chatty Cathy Doll. Also in evidence are the more traditional voodoo dolls, with inverted bowls for bodies, little petticoats underneath, and with spindly black arms and tiny black heads topped by feathers. Several people hold candles attached to plastic flowers and rum bottles covered in stripes of colored satin.

An assistant priest in nondescript old clothes begins intoning a sort of pseudo-Catholic Mass, which is a mix of Latin, French, and Creole phrases, Gregorian-type chants, and what appear to be a few pop songs thrown in for good measure. There is much crossing of selves and much sprinkling of holy water on me, my companion, and the objects we hold. There is much swinging about of a censer with incense in it that is identical to one I saw used at a coven of teenage witches in Brooklyn.

The people around me, who range in age from toddlers to the very old, are all looking at me and my elderly date and tittering. I think we must be a very hot item. Speaking of hot, I am now having a bubble bath inside my clothes. I try to take off my safari jacket and sweater and open my shirt, which takes a goodly amount of effort because my one hand is holding the sequined bottle and my other hand is still the property of Bloody Mary here.

Bloody Mary is absolutely who she is, right out of *South Pacific*, smiling her toothless black smile and saying "Iss good idea? You like?" with the little laugh at the end.

The ceremony continues. The incense pot is swung under the arms and under the feet and between the legs of a chap close to the altar who is wearing a load of beads and a very wide pimp-type hat with a rakish band and who has an insanely mean look on his face.

Apparel here tonight seems to range from threadbare

clothes to the sort of semiformal dresses that girls I went to high school with wore to dinner dances. There are several little girls wearing white dresses, there are elderly gentlemen in horn-rimmed glasses and black fedoras, and there are matronly types wearing what I imagine their equivalents in Harlem wear to church. This is, after all, church.

After about an hour of festivities at the altar, the praying stops and the drums begin again. Bloody Mary, grinning marvelously, pulls me away from the altar and toward the peristyle. Thirty or forty of the parishioners have begun to dance around it, and we join them, some of us more willingly than others.

Around and around the peristyle we go, and by now I have discarded both jacket and sweater and my shirt is open to the navel. I wonder dreamily whether, as a result of the rituals at the altar, the lady on my arm and I are engaged or married. Eugène asks me several times if I'm all right, then he slumps into a chair to rest.

Eventually Bloody Mary herself runs down and signals me to a stop. We squeeze each other and laugh and she says, "Iss good idea? You like?" and then we slump into chairs ourselves.

The drumming stops again and the witch doctor signals to somebody outside the door. Immediately, case after case of Cokes and local soft drinks are handed in over our heads, opened by the witch doctor himself, and passed around and drunk.

Eugène asks me how long I want to stay. I say I don't really know—what's coming up next?"

"More donceeng," says Eugène.

"Oh yeah?" I say. "How much more?"

Eugène turns to the fellow next to him and asks him.

"About eight, nine hours more of donceeng," says Eugène.

Good God! In eight or nine more hours of dancing around the peristyle I'd end up as a puddle of melted butter, just like the tigers in *Little Black Sambo*.

Eugène asks if it would be all right to go, and I say yes. We bid goodbye to the natty witch doctor and to Bloody Mary, and we squeeze our way out of the temple and into the night. Eugène unlocks the car, and we drive tiredly back to the hotel.

"What were they going to sacrifice?" I say.

"A cheecken, a peeg, a goat, porhops a cow," says Eugène.

The prospect of watching animals being butchered a foot away from me in a crowded, hot, and airless space is enough to make me nauseous in itself. I am not at all sorry to be missing it.

"Lost night," says Eugène, "I take some people to de place I take you de first night you came. Was a good socrifice lost night."

"Oh?" I say. "What did they sacrifice?"

"A peeg," says Eugène.

"How did they kill it?" I say without thinking.

"De mon he ees possessed, he bite de peeg on de face," says Eugène.

"He bite de peeg on de face?" I say. Somehow this doesn't sound terribly lethal.

"De mon keep biting de peeg on de face and on de throat until he die," Eugène explains.

I begin to get the picture, unfortunately, and I don't really want to know the answer to the next question but it's hopped right out of my mouth before I can stop it.

"How long did it take the pig to die?" I say.

"About maybe twenty, thirty minute," says Eugène. "Very good socrifice."

AND so it was that I went to three voodoo ceremonies in Haiti and took part in two of them, at least one and three-fourths of which were real, and lived to tell about it. And so it was that none of the dark things warned about by my friends ever came to pass.

And so it was that somebody I know called me only two weeks after I came back and said that he was thinking of going to Haiti himself.

"Let me tell you about Haiti," I said eagerly. "First of all, the minute you get off the plane there, the sense of evil of the place will envelop you like a warm bath. . . . "

In Haiti, by day or by night, you cannot escape the sound of voodoo drums. In Sandstone, by day or by night, you cannot escape the sound of people having flashy orgasms. I have been both places, heard both sounds, and I am here to tell you that the drums are neither as prevalent nor as noisy as the orgasms.

Sandstone, in case you hadn't heard, is an idyllic mountaintop retreat in Topanga, California, just north of Los Angeles, where few if any clothes are worn, where neither sexual nor toilet functions go on behind closed doors (primarily because at Sandstone there *aren't* many doors, closed or otherwise), and where it is thought a fine thing to have one close Primary sexual relationship and several what they call Satellite ones.

I had planned at this point to tell you how the nasty old editors at *Playboy*, knowing how shy I am, dragged me kicking and screaming to the gates of Sandstone and threw me inside. It would have been a blue-eyed bald-faced lie. As a matter of fact, I think it's high time I made a confession to you: every article I've written in these pages in which I personally investigated some area of tacky sex—like going to an orgy or answering kinky sex ads—has not been, as I've suggested, the fiendish scheme of a sadistic editor but an idea thought up by your correspondent himself. I just thought you ought to know that.

Oh, the shyness and the fright I described in those articles were absolutely genuine, you needn't worry about *that*. But I did feel it was time I dropped the pretense that researching such stories is a job akin to mining anthracite.

Very well then. With this new bond of frankness and trust between us, perhaps we are better equipped to share an adventure as intimate as Sandstone.

As OUR story opens, we find shy but eager Greenburg arriving at Sandstone late on the afternoon of Friday, July 2, 1976, after a scenic but chilling drive through tricky mountain passes, for a weekend of patriotic Bicentennial fun. With me in the car is an equally shy, if not as eager, Primary whom I shall call Judy, largely because that is her name. Judy has made it abundantly clear to me that she intends neither to bed down with anyone at Sandstone but this reporter, nor to wear anything scantier than a bikini. Yet, should it become absolutely necessary, she stands willing to observe others doing whatever they feel they must.

We park the car and walk up the hill from the parking lot to the main building, where we are to be interviewed to determine our suitability as Sandstone guests. As our story progresses and you begin to get an idea of how intimate people get with each other at Sandstone, you will perhaps see the wisdom of any process designed to weed out, say, advanced ringworm cases and necrophiliacs.

In the courtyard of the main building is a pond filled with rocks and moss and giant Japanese goldfish. A splashing fountain in the pond provides the only audible sound so far. Beyond the main building can be seen the Pacific Ocean, covered with a layer of cottony clouds. Sandstone is well above the clouds.

We enter the main building and find ourselves in a large living room with a high ceiling, several sofa seating areas, a fireplace, and sliding glass doors that open onto an elevated deck. Stained-glass windows adjoining the sliding glass doors prove upon close examination to be illustrations of couples in the most popular coital positions, interspersed with idealized close-ups of the male and female sex organs.

A clothed gentleman and a naked woman with pendulous breasts beckon us to sit down, share a glass of fruit juice, and fill out entry forms. As Judy and I are drinking our fruit juice and filling out our forms we see another couple enter, greet the clothed man and the naked woman, and also begin filling out forms. Although the couple appear quite intimate, the gentleman misspells his Primary's name on her entry card.

At length Judy and I are ushered into a small office adjoining the living room. Our interviewer is a darkly attractive and petite young woman named Pam, who used to be assistant couture buyer at Saks Fifth Avenue and who is now Manager of the Sandstone Club, which is Sandstone's social section. The other two parts of Sandstone are the Community—the resident "family" of about two dozen staff members—and the Center, which is the educational division of Sandstone and which sponsors seminars and workshops with such bouncy titles as "Open Relationships, Advanced," "Bioenergy for Fun and Prophet," "Fear of Rejection," "Being Bisexual," "Massage for Lovers and Friends," "Developing Chutzpah: Assertiveness Training," and "Pathways to Sensuality," in which "Alternate styles of tumescing are demonstrated."

In the interview we learn that Sandstone was founded in 1967 by engineer John Williamson and his wife Barbara, was closed and reopened a couple of times following a massive forest fire in 1970 and a gigantic legal battle with the Los Angeles Board of Supervisors, who couldn't bear the thought of all those naked folks up there having so much fun together. Sandstone was finally taken over in 1973 by Dr. Paul Paige, an attractive young marriage counselor, Gestalt therapist, and ex-Marine. For the next three years, Sandstone enjoyed legal and financial health. It attracted an impressive number of physicians, psychologists, professors, and horny people, including *Joy of Sex* author Dr. Alex Comfort, writer Gay Talese, TV personality Orson Bean, and prestigious *New York Times* cultural editor Max Lerner.

Pam warns us that the following are verboten at Sandstone: booze, illegal drugs, children under eighteen, pets, and hostile or abusive behavior. Fortunately we have brought none of these in with us, with the possible exception of a smallish flask filled with, I forget now, either vodka, gerbils, or sarcasm. Pam further warns us of some of the outdoor dangers at Sandstone—rattlesnakes and tarantulas—but it's the *indoor* ones that I personally find more threatening, like blundering into breaches of sexual protocol and like encountering ensemble sexual rejection.

Pam says that although sexual activity can and does take place in any part of Sandstone, most of it is centered in the two rooms on the main building's lower floor. The Playroom is an immense room lined with king-sized mattresses and water beds. Couples interested in one-on-one sex predominate in the Playroom. Those with a penchant for multiple couplings tend to hang out more in the smaller, split-leveled Ballroom next door.

If we should find ourselves in the Ballroom and be intrigued with the notion of participating in the activities of any ongoing group, Pam explains, the protocol is to touch one of the participants of the group lightly on the arm. He or she will thereupon either wave us away or pull us into the group.

Pam says that most men when they first come to Sandstone experience two phenomena: (1) what Sandstone regulars refer to as the kid-in-the-candy-store syndrome, or what I call The

Heartbreak of Satyriasis, and (2) impotence. Neither of these, says Pam consolingly, lasts very long—usually no longer than a month. Women, says Pam, tend at first to find it difficult to refuse any man who wants to do it with them—what Sandstone regulars call "mercy-fucking." The other noteworthy term that Pam uses and that we will hear a lot during our weekend stay is "down the hill"—Sandstone members' mildly patronizing term for the rest of the world outside Sandstone.

The main events this weekend are an all-day seminar-workshop called "The Sandstone Experience," and a special Saturday night party, whence most sexual activity of a scheduled nature takes place. Attending the seminar-workshop is largely a matter of paying an enrollment fee. Attending the Saturday night party is a matter of getting a personal invitation after one is looked over and deemed suitable. It is not clear to us at this point what makes one suitable, it is only clear that *not* to be found suitable is going to be rather unpleasant should it occur.

Although Judy informs Pam of her reluctance to either copulate with strangers or to disrobe, Pam does not seem to be dismayed. She concludes our interview, which we appear to have passed, and tells us that we can now pay our fees of $50 per person per day (or $200 for two days) if we wish, and even if we don't wish. And then she ushers us to the Pong Room, so named because it is adjacent to the outdoor Ping-Pong table, where we shall be spending Friday and Saturday nights. The Pong Room is one of the only two private guest rooms with doors at Sandstone, other guests being obliged to sleep communally in the Playroom and Ballroom, cuddled up together like litters of kittens. It does not occur to me until it is too late that sleeping cuddled up like kittens with an informal group of ladies and gents in the Playroom or Ballroom might be preferable to sleeping in the Pong Room, which is not only adjacent to the Ping-Pong table but to the kitchen, whose activities begin in the vicinity of dawn.

After writing Pam a check for $200, we make our way out of the understated simplicity of the Pong Room's lumpy convertible sofa to the parking lot to get our bags. There we are confronted by an affable yet not altogether reputable looking chap who asks us if we are swingers.

We say no, and the affable chap says that's O.K., no problem, he just happened to be in the neighborhood and decided to check this Sandstone place out, he being a swinger himself and having heard a good deal about the thing and having also been a member for quite a few years of a similar place not far from here called Elysium Fields—had we heard of it?—here was his Elysium membership card right here, see, same type of place, really, except that there were young kids on the premises so you couldn't fuck right outside, but otherwise about the same, and he'd been hanging out at Elysium for quite a while, as he'd said, although he was tired of the place, felt Elysium was a little too, well, intense for him, the relationships one got into there were a little too deep, since what he really liked to do best was to go into a bar and pick up some broad and throw her a fuck, begging Judy's pardon for his French and hoping she wasn't offended.

Judy indicates she is not offended, at least not by the word fuck, and I manage to extricate us from his nonstop affability long enough to grab our bags out of the car and run. The gentleman, it seems, has also just been interviewed by Pam and (one begins to see the wisdom in such things) failed to pass.

THAT NIGHT there is an astonishingly good buffet dinner of fishkabob in a creamy white wine sauce and broccoli with hollandaise, and a mixed consciousness-raising session in the Playroom in which seventeen clothed people attempt to raise their consciousness on the topic "Dignity and Privacy in Sex."

Usually consciousness-raising sessions are segregated by sex here, but tonight's is not, due to the small turnout of guests. In a recent women's c-r session here, it came out that most ladies didn't really know what other ladies' vaginas looked like, much less their own, and so they turned up the lights and turned down their panties and looked inside each other and poked around in there until they got a real sense of the thing, and a guy who was passing in the hall peeked in and asked what was going on and was told that they were examining vaginas and did he want to take a look, and he said sure and came in for a gander as well.

Our group leader asks what Dignity and Privacy in Sex means to us. One woman says, "To me it means that when I am fucking some guy in the Ballroom my husband feels free to come and join in with us, but not when I am fucking somebody in the Playroom. Then he is discreet and stays away."

Someone else says that to him it means that a couple can have a go at it on the front lawn as one couple did here quite recently, and everyone respected their privacy and paid not the least bit of attention to them, with the one teeny exception that, at the moment of the couple's mutual and not inaudible orgasm, everybody burst into applause.

There is much talk of a somewhat self-congratulatory nature about the seriousness of the Sandstone phenomenon, its larger ramifications for the society as a whole, blah blah blah, and some young upstart of a Singles guest—Friday night is the only night that Singles are allowed at Sandstone without partners—says that this is all a lot of hooey and why can't anybody admit that Sandstone is nothing but a fuck club. Everybody leaps on the guy and has a lot of salty things to say to him, and if one thing is sure it is that this guy is a snap not to be invited to the Saturday Night Party.

After the c-r session we drift upstairs. I am hoping there will be some sort of sexual activity scheduled, but what there is is a couple of young entertainers singing and playing the guitar very sweetly, and one or two informal rap sessions, also clothed.

I meet a guy named Mitch who is in his mid-thirties and who is a group therapist and a sculptor. With Mitch is an attractive blonde girl, very slender, name of Susan. Susan is twenty-eight, is a dental hygienist and a struggling stand-up comedienne. She is also Mitch's Primary. They live together at the beach in Santa Monica and have an open relationship, which means they allow each other to have sleep-over dates with other people.

Both Mitch and Susan claim to have outgrown all feelings of jealousy regarding each other's Satellites. Both have been members of Sandstone for several years. Both have matched sets of Jewish parents who are mortified by the whole notion of Sandstone and of open relationships, Susan's refusing even to claim her as a daughter altogether for the first two years they knew about it. (Both Mitch and Susan are named things other than Mitch and Susan; they have asked me to disguise them in this article to save their parents further migranes and peptic ulcers.)

Mitch and Susan are equally endowed with a strong sense of humor, but Susan's is initially too acidic for my taste and so I spend the bulk of my time with Mitch who has the greater warmth. Mitch and Susan leave early and say they'll be back tomorrow night. I have good feelings about both of them, especially about Mitch. If we lived in the same city we'd probably be friends.

After they go I strike up a lively conversation with a lovely plump grandmotherly lady with schoolmarmish steel-rimmed glasses and white hair piled up in a bun. She tells me that she is, indeed, a schoolmarm, for prekindergarteners, and that she and her husband came to Sandstone after twenty-five years of wedded bliss, and they are still blissfully wedded. The members and guests at Sandstone are of all ages, from their twenties through their sixties, and we will meet many this weekend who claim to have been happily married for that long, and a few not so happily who came here after a quarter of a century of matrimony to save their marriages.

A fellow on my left, hearing me express surprise at the number of oldsters who seem willing to frisk about in the altogether, tells me he once brought his seventy-five-year-old mother up to Sandstone for a visit.

"When she finally got around to taking off her clothes," he says, "two young girls in their twenties came up to her and began admiring her boobs and fondling them and saying what great shape they were in."

By about one a.m. it is apparent to me that nothing more promising than stories about the handling of granny jugs is in the offing, so Judy and I retire to the Pong Room for a little Dignity and Privacy in Sex. Subsequent trips to the closest bathrooms prove unfulfilling—small groups of lallygaggers loiter at the doorways and there are no doors to shield me from them. Not being one who is comfortable performing toilet functions as a spectator sport, I elect to hold it in till morning. It is not clear to me why Sandstone's open-door policy on sexual activity extends to the bathroom, but I guess that's just East Coast muddleheadedness on my part.

Morning produces no more private opportunities for Dignity and Privacy in Toilet than the previous night, and so I am forced to enter a restroom clotted with amiable bathroomgoers and stand in line with both men and women to use the commode. I take turns admiring the wallpaper, which is patterned with stylized couples in top-forty conjugal positions, and studying the aplomb of the various pishers who precede me in line. The last person ahead of me is an attractive lady of about forty who looks like she's been doing such things all her life. She sits down on the seat, pulls down her panties and does one of the less ruffled sissies I have ever seen.

When she is finished I stride to the john and, mustering

as much nonchalance as I can, unzip, dig out my shvantz and execute one of the three most casual weewees of the day. (I am to participate in many such communal urinations this weekend, but somehow I shall never make the quantum leap to communal defacations. Self-critical as I may be, I do not find this to be a serious flaw in my character.)

Right after breakfast, two dozen of us meet clothed for a rap session in the Playroom, which is the formal beginning of the day-long Sandstone Experience Seminar-Workshop. Everybody in the group introduces himself and gives a brief biographical sketch. There are two M.D.s, one of whom just kicked a dexie addiction he picked up years ago in med school. There are a couple of lawyers, a couple of shrinks, several housewives, one phone company executive and one gas company one, three engineers, three writers, a professor of musicology, and a chiropractor. I decide to be out front about the article I'm writing, which makes everybody instantly self-conscious and quippy.

Paul Paige, Sandstone's mentor, discusses with us the exquisite philosophical distinctions between Balling, Fucking, and Making Love, and between Sexuality and Sensuality, none of which at this point I understand. There is a brief tour of the grounds, the buildings, and the outdoor Jacuzzi. "Three women have left their husbands for the nozzles on this thing," says our guide, and everyone chuckles in anticipation. We are shown the private bungalows occupied by Paul and Pam, where for some reason they choose to get in an occasional private act of either sex or ca-ca—Do As I Say, Not As I Doo-doo?—and then we are ushered into the building that houses Sandstone's incredible Olympic-sized indoor pool with body-temperature water and are given an opportunity to undress.

Only Judy, of the two dozen seminar-workshop members, elects to remain clothed. The rest of us slip out of our duds, hang them on hooks on the wall, and enter the very warm and surprisingly erotic water. Several of the men are wearing gold chains around their necks. Several of the women are wearing gold chains around their waists and some around their ankles. Judy observes to me later that there appears to be in Southern California a relationship between nudity and ornamentation. "The less clothing, the more body jewelry," she says.

We are instructed to form a large circle in the waist-deep part of the pool. Then one person at a time lies down in the water on his back, closes his eyes, and trusts the rest of us to keep his head out of the water as we float him slowly around the circle. As each person is passed around, there are occasional light random caresses of the trusting person's body, though not in the genital region. When it is time for me to be floated around the circle, I find it a wonderfully peaceful and lovely experience.

The second exercise finds us forming two straight parallel lines in the pool, again passing one floating and trusting person after another down the line. This time there is more activity on the part of the passers. There is some light stroking of breasts and of pudenda. One fellow asks that we hum to stimulate his eardrums underwater as he passes us. Another, an apparent foot fetishist, persistently reaches out for and sucks on any passing toes in the vicinity of his mouth. Yet another finds himself bending to kiss and lick an occasional female nipple.

The third exercise finds us forming two concentric circles, joining hands, and closing eyes. At a signal from our leader, the outer circle, of which I am presently not a part, begins moving and, at another signal, stops. With no eyes being opened, each person in the outer circle then feels around for the person in front of him and begins stroking his or her body.

The first time I realize that hard masculine hands are caressing my back and chest and shoulders I feel quite uncomfortable. It seems to me that, were I to find myself enjoying being fondled by a man, I would burst into full fag-hood and become an instant hairdresser—Mr. Dan, giving limp-wristed wash-and-sets. As it continues, and no hair rollers sprout from my palms, I begin to relax and I decide that it is not inappropriate to be thus stroked, particularly since no genital areas seem to be involved. The group leader repeatedly tells us to take responsibility for communicating with our bodies what we wish or don't wish our fondlers to do to us.

When the outer circle has completed a full tour of the inner one, we exchange places, and our group has an opportunity to caress theirs. Once again, the first time I reach out for the body ahead of mine and feel not the familiar smooth shape of a lady but that of a hard, hairy, heavily-muscled man, I am initially uncomfortable. And once again, finding no hairdressing salons materializing around me, I relax and decide it is O.K. for me to pat a male body.

To my extreme disappointment, the bodies I find in front of me as I move blindly around the circle seem to be more men than women. To my further disappointment our group leader soon indicates it is high time we open our eyes, climb out of the water, and go to have lunch. I am the last to leave the pool.

I stand drying myself off and dressing and I notice that alongside me is another of Sandstone's famous doorless bathrooms. On the can is a guy from our workshop having a rather noisy b.m. and giving a running commentary on the state of his bowels.

I beat a hasty retreat and make my way over to Judy, who has participated in this morning's activities from a safe, clothed, arid vantage point. Judy assures me she intends to continue being safe, clothed, and arid. I tell her she really missed something by not being in the pool.

"Yeah," she says. "I also missed World War II and I'm not sorry about that either."

I figure everything in the second half of the seminar is going to be anticlimactic after the morning activities in the pool. I figure wrong.

The first thing we do after lunch is a massage workshop. Three narrow folding massage tables have been set up end to end in the Playroom. Everybody in the twenty-four-member group takes off his or her clothes, except for Judy and except for one guy with white hair who keeps his socks and shoes on because, he says, he is recovering from a cold.

One person gets up on each massage table and lies down. The rest of us form a circle around the three tables. We are handed several bottles of appealingly scented oil and are instructed to pour great quantities of same upon the bodies in front of us and to rub it into their skins. At a signal from our leader the recumbent bodies close their eyes and the upright ones begin moving in a clockwise direction around the tables, massaging the bodies in the same way we're moving.

If there was only light petting above the waist in the pool, there is now very definite heavy petting both above and below the waist on the tables. Oddly, none of the men appear to be getting erections. A bearded professor of musicology who had in the morning rap session used a number of polysyllabic words like "perjorative" and who consistently referred to his privates as "genitalia" says that in the pool he was sad that nobody touched his genitalia, and now that they were it felt good and he wished that he had an erection so as to call further attention to them. "Call attention to *what?*" someone asks.

"To my . . . cock," he replies.

Everybody applauds.

Before long all the men, including me, have touched the flaccid penises of the gentlemen on the tables we passed. It is an odd sensation. One man observes that other men's penises feel softer and more fragile than his own, and everyone concurs. One lady observes that she finds the same true about the breasts she's been touching.

"You can sit around all day touching your breasts," she says, "but they just don't feel the same as someone else's."

Finally it gets to be my turn on the table. I close my eyes and the hands begin a tour of my body. Up the right side, down the left. Someone rubs my penis. So does someone else. And someone else. And several someone elses. It feels weird. And marvelous. Twenty-one people, forty-two hands, all massaging me, stroking me, fondling me, caressing me, loving me up. It's as if an entire committee suddenly fell unanimously in love with me and asked nothing more than the opportunity of expressing its affection. It's as if a forty-two-handed sea creature were trying to seduce me. "It's like passing through a human car wash," says a man on the next table.

The massage is supposed to last three minutes. It is impossible to say how long it actually takes. Like the other men, I don't have an erection during the massage. It seems somehow appropriate not to. It would also seem appropriate were I to get one. I feel for the first time here a great sense of relaxation, and suddenly I realize that I know the difference between sexuality and sensuality, that this is the latter, with no expectations about performance on me, with no anxieties about doing the right or wrong thing. It is very nice, very nice indeed.

When it is over the massagees are supposed to tell the massagers what it was like for them. I tell the massagers a bit about the above, about getting the difference between sexuality and sensuality and all the rest of it, and then I tell them I'd like to room with all of them next semester—an old Kingston Trio line, but it pleases them.

Eventually we all have had our turns on the tables, one or two of us may have even snuck in a second turn, and we are all glistening and oozing and dripping with perfumed oil. The group leader says there will be a break for showers and then we will reconvene for a rap session in the Ballroom.

I walk into the oversize shower room with three men and

a lady. The lady is about 30, dark, attractive, nicely shaped. The lady is rubbing soap on one of the men, who looks a bit like Jimmy Carter. Then the lady starts rubbing soap on me, on my back. It feels nice and I thank her. The lady smiles and begins rubbing soap into my sexual equipment. As she does this she looks at me and says as follows: "Hi, my name is Sharon and I would like to be mentioned in the article you are writing for *Playboy*."

"Sharon," I say, "you got it."

Whereupon I lean over and plant a nice kiss on her lips, whereupon her lips part, whereupon I slip my tongue in between them. Sharon shivers, startled, as if all this massaging of peepees was just in fun but tongues in mouths are serious stuff. Perhaps tongues in mouths in Sandstone shower rooms are inappropriate. Perhaps everyone is merely holding back, saving it for tonight, saving themselves for the big Saturday Night Blast.

When Sharon pulls away, I open my eyes and notice that the chap standing just in back of her is the big guy who looks like Jimmy Carter and who is evidently the lady's husband. I know that I have done nothing really out of line, that Sharon's hubby is as conversant as I am with Sandstone's policy of Primaries and Satellites and all, but still there is a little something in how he is looking at me, and I decide to flash him a quick smile and beat it out of the shower room.

The rap session in the Ballroom is the concluding phase of the all-day workshop. In it everyone shares their impressions of the day and how the experience matched up to their expectations of it.

The guy who wore his socks and shoes in the massage workshop tells Judy he resents the fact that she wore her clothes throughout the seminar and didn't participate with the rest of us. Everybody jumps on him, saying she *did* participate, but on the level she felt comfortable with, that that was just as valid as the way in which *he* had participated, that that was called taking care of oneself and that that was to be not attacked but admired.

It's beautiful. Judy herself is so grateful for the group's reaction she is on the verge of tears. She thanks them and says that she does feel she participated with them in the activities and she also says that she has never had such a warm and supportive reaction from a group in her life.

The seminar ends. Judy and I return to the Pong Room. I tell her about the incident in the shower with Sharon. She seems inordinately interested in hearing about it.

We dress for dinner, still not knowing whether we are invited to the big party afterward. Like the story about the man with the flat tire who's walking to the gas station in the boondocks and worrying how much he's going to be charged for the jack and getting madder and madder in anticipation, I begin to fantasize demeaning conversations in which I am told that, for whatever reason, Judy and I are not invited to the party.

I walk into the main living room and try to find someone who knows if we're invited, but all I manage to do is find out some of the people who have *not* been invited: the guy who wore his socks and didn't approve of Judy being clothed has not been invited; the guy who said Sandstone was nothing more than a fuck club has not, of course, been invited; a very tall psychiatrist with strange red hair and a strange red mephistophelian beard who'd been spotted playfully trying to drown some of the young ladies in the pool in this morning's exercises has most emphatically been not invited.

There has been a lot of talk about how everybody who stays for the party must have a partner of the opposite sex available to others, and I worry that Judy's known policy of abstinence, no matter how much it is officially cheered as Judy taking care of herself, may have disqualified us.

I finally manage to seek out a Sandstone official and, eyes smoldering, demand to know if we are invited or not to the goddamned party. Yes, he says, we are. We are? Really? Oh. How nice.

Dinner Saturday night is again buffet style. Judy and I heap our plates and then look around for someone to sit down with. There are perhaps thirty or forty people in their thirties and forties sitting about in the living room and out on the deck, most of them fairly attractive looking. Two outrageously wholesome and pretty California girls with long blonde hair pass by us and I wonder idly if I will be having intimate dealings with them later on tonight, singly or—my great fantasy—in a threesome, and how one goes about arranging such things.

I spot Sharon and her husband sitting on the deck and point them out to Judy. To my surprise she suggests we sit down with them. We do. And when it is time for dessert, both Sharon and Judy get up and bring it back for us, and when they return they are both smiling in a peculiar manner.

"Judy tells me that the thing in the shower really turned you on," says Sharon.

I admit that it did.

"It turned me on too," says Sharon. She flashes a quick look at Judy and then continues. "I told Judy I really wanted to make it with you and asked her if she minded. Judy said she liked me and that if you had to do it with anyone here she'd prefer it was with me."

I nod and flash a fast look at Judy and then at Sharon's husband. Sharon's husband's face is betraying nothing at all, but he and Sharon are looking at each other and it is a cinch that as many messages are going back and forth between them as pass through any Western Union office on Mother's Day.

"So," says Sharon, "would you like to come downstairs with me?"

"When?" I say.

"How about right now?" says Sharon.

I look at Sharon a moment, then at Judy, then at Sharon's husband, then back at Sharon.

"Now is fine," I say and get up and, with more rapid glances and a few quickee smiles at both, I take Sharon's hand and follow her downstairs to the Playroom for dessert.

Outside the Playroom is a little anteroom with lockers and towels and a couple of racks for hanging clothes. Sharon and I swiftly slip out of everything but our underpants, agreeing we find this sexier than starting out totally naked, and then we enter the Playroom.

In the faint light we can see bodies rhythmically rising and falling, and the ever-present cries of lovers in the throes of unimaginable ecstasy provide a suitable chorus of greeting. Although dinner upstairs has scarcely concluded, at least six couples have already begun strenuous workouts on the mats, being obviously unaware of the warning I was given as a kid, that rigorous exercise immediately after eating gives you cramps.

Sharon and I make our way to the end of the Playroom to a vacant king-sized mattress in the corner, lie down and begin foreplay. If the sounds of lovemaking on all sides of me are not necessarily a stimulant, neither, surprisingly, are they a deterrent, and soon our voices blend with theirs in some primitive tribal call of the wild.

When we have finished, we are breathless and pleased with ourselves and with each other, and not yet sated. I suggest a visit to the pool and Sharon assents. We pick our way back through the bodies in the Playroom which, like machinery in Southern California oil fields, has never ceased its regular and relentless up-and-down activity. We don minimal clothing against the chill night air and make our way across the unlit grounds to the pool house.

The pool house is deserted and dark. Without turning on any lights, we slip naked into the 93° F. water and embrace. I have attempted underwater lovemaking on a few previous occasions—at night in a semi-public swimming pool in Mexico and in the daytime in both the Caribbean and the Atlantic

Ocean—and at no time was it any more than a zany adventure and a barely lubricated and, hence, moderately painful proposition. Tonight, with an already slippery Sharon in the hot waters of the Sandstone pool, submerged sex comes of age.

If God himself had appeared to me then and said, "All right, Greenburg, that's it—a little fun is *one* thing, but you've gone and abused the privilege and that's the 3–0 mark for life on Earth," I would have found it entirely reasonable and gone along quietly.

Sharon and I proceed from the pool house to the outdoor Jacuzzi which, though hot and bubbling, is not going to make either of us leave our mates for one of its nozzles. When I suggest to Sharon that we drop into the Ballroom to see whether anyone has any openings on their dance cards, Sharon replies that she really isn't up for it, that she really is beginning to worry that we have been gone too long and that her husband might be getting restless.

"Frankly," says Sharon, "about the only thing I'd be the slightest bit interested in at this point is a threesome with another girl."

If my teeth were not firmly anchored to my jaws they would have surely fallen out and clattered to the deck of the Jacuzzi.

"Are you *serious* about that?" I say.

Sharon looks puzzled.

"Sure I'm serious," she says. "Why?"

"I really *have* died and gone to Heaven," I say. "A threesome with two women just happens to be my longest-running unfulfilled fantasy."

Sharon smiles at the notion that anything so attainable could possibly be anybody's fantasy and suggests I look around for a lady I want to be our third partner.

I have not gotten far into looking when we come across Sharon's hubby. We *have* been gone a long time, and I feel a bit peculiar seeing him and look the other way and busy myself with the belt of my bush jacket. Sharon's hubby must be feeling a bit peculiar too, judging by how much he looks like he is *not* feeling peculiar. Sharon says she will go and talk to him awhile and that I should keep looking for our third partner, and then she goes off with her husband.

I go back to the main living room and find Judy and ask her how she is doing. Judy says she is doing O.K., so I drift away and continue looking around for girls for our threesome, but there do not seem to be any loose ones around and it soon becomes apparent that Sharon is very much no longer around herself.

It is starting to get late. I have had an incredible time with Sharon and now it is over and for some reason I find that I am still hungry. How, after all the stuff I did with her, could I possibly be feeling this way? Maybe it's that I haven't yet gotten my threesome, nor found my way to the floor of the Ballroom. Maybe it's simply what they call up here the old kid-in-the-candy-store syndrome.

I chat with the attractive staff member named Annette who had enrolled me in today's seminar-workshop about the seminar-workshop, about the difference between sexuality and sensuality, about changing sexual mores and the ramifications of the Sandstone experience on the society as a whole, about threesomes, about how Annette feels about threesomes, about how Annette doesn't go in for threesomes, about how Annette feels about maybe popping down to the Playroom for a fast twosome.

Annette says she's already had enough sex for one night, thanks, besides which her date is feeling a little neglected because she left him alone to go downstairs awhile ago with somebody else and she really feels she ought to go and find him and see how he is. But I persist and Annette relents and we do go down to the Playroom for some spirited if not lengthy lovemaking, at the conclusion of which she bounds upstairs to make sure her date is O.K. I amble back upstairs and prowl about wearing just my bush jacket—a hunter on a sexual safari who has found the spoor but not yet bagged his limit.

Judy is getting restless and wants to go to bed. Sharon has not reappeared. Mitch and Susan do not seem to have made it back up the hill for the party. I don't quite know what it is I want, but I know I haven't found it yet. Judy goes off to bed. I continue prowling.

A darkly beautiful and very young married girl named Dianne sits on a couch in the living room with her husband and two other couples, laughing. I normally can't stand strangers anywhere sitting and laughing—I always think it is me they are laughing at—but now is not normally and so I sit down and join them. They are polite but seemingly into their own thing, whatever it is, and so I end up feeling slightly foolish and leave.

In the kitchen I am surprised to run into Susan. She and Mitch got here awhile ago, looked around for me without success, and now Mitch has disappeared somewhere, Susan doesn't know where. Susan is wearing jeans, no top, and a pair of small yet perky breasts with pert pink nipples. Looking at them I feel myself getting turned on and wonder whether, in view of my new friendship with Mitch, this feeling is appropriate.

Susan seems tired, willing to talk, less acidic, and not discernibly interested in making love. I figure it's probably just as well. We stand in the kitchen, leaning against the counter and drinking somebody's too-sweet jug wine, and compare notes about the stand-up comedy biz—five years ago I had a stand-up comedy act with partner Avery Corman and I sympathize with anybody who is similarly obsessed.

The perplexing thing is that, inappropriateness notwithstanding, the more Susan and I talk the more I want to make it with her. At length I elect to bring the matter out into the open.

"Susan," I say, "I feel slightly disloyal even mentioning this, but here I am talking about comedy routines when what I am mainly doing is studying your remarkable breasts. I know you and Mitch don't have any qualms about such things, but the fact that you're his Primary prevents me from even suggesting that we go downstairs together."

Note the sneakiness here of using the notion that I have philosophical difficulties with making a pass at my friend's mate as the actual pass itself.

Susan fails to respond in the fashion I'd anticipated, fails to draw me to her bosom and assure me I'll soon learn Sandstone's loosey-goosey lifestyle, and it takes a while longer before I am able, under the pretext of doing a little harmless hugging, to turn her on and persuade her to come and play with me in the Playroom.

The whole time we are down there I am wondering what I will say if Mitch shows up. I tell Susan what I am wondering and she assures me that there isn't any problem, he will just whisper "Susan, are you all right?" and she will whisper "Yes," and then he will go and wait outside.

We finish making love and Mitch has, fortunately, not shown up. I am relieved. I am also perversely disappointed. I feel somehow that I would like to have the experience of being assured by Mitch that it is O.K. with him for me to have had sex with his girlfriend.

We go upstairs to find Mitch. But Mitch is not upstairs, nor is hardly anyone upstairs at this late hour. Susan goes off to look for Mitch and I go off finally to the Pong Room and bed.

Judy is in bed but not asleep. I sit down on the bed, feeling a little strange. Strange about the fact that I have made love to three other women tonight and that Judy not only gave permission for same but actually set up the first one. Would I have been so permissive with Judy, especially if we had been deeply involved with one another, married or even living together, told her to go ahead, fuck any guy you want, even spoken to someone she seemed turned on by and told him that it was O.K. for him to fuck her? Not in a male chauvinist pig's eye would I.

But if it's all right for me to have other women, then why isn't it all right for a woman of mine to have other men?

Why, outside of the fact that, despite the best of intentions to the contrary, I still seem to have strong gut reactions to macho and to the double standard and to all the rest of that nonsense which, although nonsense, continues to have a profound influence on my life.

Judy doesn't press me for details of the night's safari and I am glad. We lie together and hug and then, although I am by now exhausted and my member is chafed from friction with assorted places it's been tonight and although I am developing an odd sense of *déjà vu*, we still somehow manage to complete the act and fall asleep.

SUNDAY. Sunday is very low key. Although it is the Fourth of July, the nation's two hundredth birthday, there is surprisingly not a single *double-entendre* about it or bangs or whatever. Contrary to some of the things I have thus far chosen to tell you about Sandstone, the folks up here are not only smarter and more articulate than I had expected, they also—wonder of wonders—have a fairly nice sense of humor about themselves as well.

The sun is hot and about twenty of us, mostly nude, lie out on the sun deck together. I am only slightly worried about the dangers of a tricky sunburn on areas not already tanned. One man tells of a time he had a painfully sunburned scrotum.

"Oh, there's nothing worse than sunburned nipples," replies a lady who evidently has some expertise in that area. There follows a good deal of idle speculation about whether the sensitive skin of the nipples is the same as that of the scrotum or penis. Somebody is using a brand of suntan oil which smells like coconuts. We all help ourselves to liberal splashes of it and rub it primarily into our nipples, scrotums and penises, and soon we are all smelling like one big macaroon.

I have a lingering uneasy feeling which is in part due to the fact that I have yet to talk to Mitch about the experience with Susan. I ask whether anyone has seen Mitch or Susan around today, but no one has.

Directly below my position at the rail of the sun deck is the Jacuzzi. In it are Paul Paige and a number of people in a workshop he is running. For over an hour I watch successive members of his group being suspended in the warm water of the Jacuzzi with eyes closed, being held and hugged and fondled. The experience evidently causes many of them to have flashes of a happier interuterine life and to weep softly. I could weep softly myself, thinking about my own interuterine experience in the pool last night.

Meanwhile, back on the deck, a young man lies down alongside a pretty young woman who is half asleep on her stomach and begins gently fingerfucking her. This activity continues for perhaps thirty minutes. The young lady breaks into wracking orgasmic sobs just as Pam appears, leading a middle-aged friend of her mother's whom she is showing around the place. Pam's mother's friend, being no fool, is instantly impressed with the place and elects to stick around.

Sharon and her husband have not reappeared. I commend Judy on the incredible generosity she displayed in fixing me up with Sharon at dinner. I hadn't expected her feelings about me to permit such generosity.

"I didn't really do it out of generosity," says Judy.

"You didn't?" I say.

"No," says Judy. "I fixed you up with Sharon to get you away from those two great-looking blondes with the long silky hair you were looking at when we came into dinner. I figured Sharon was at least married and a known quantity."

LATER ON in the afternoon I spot Mitch. With mounting apprehension I make my way over to him and, without even saying hello, I blurt out the following:

"Mitch, I just wanted to tell you that I made love to Susan last night and I know you probably know that because she told you and I know it's probably at least theoretically O.K. with you but I just wanted to be sure that it *is* O.K. with you."

"Susan *did* tell me," says Mitch, smiling, "and it *is* O.K. with me. Susan said you were very nice."

"Well, so was *Susan* very nice," I say, "and so are you, Mitch, I really mean that. And this is one of the strangest conversations I've ever had in my life."

WE LEFT Sandstone late Sunday night, long after the appropriate departure hour. I walked backward all the way to the Pong Room to pack and all the way to the parking lot, hoping perhaps that somebody would beckon me back. I did not want to leave, I really didn't. And I want to go back.

I miss the curiously free and intimate feeling of walking around without clothing. I miss the low-key sensuality that pervades the place. I miss Sharon and Annette and Dianne and Susan and Mitch and Pam and Paul and I miss the committee who fell in love with me. For some curious reason I even miss the relentless and yet strangely reassuring sound of people having constant flashy orgasms, and I have lately taken to listening to the more contrived ones on the Donna Summer record albums.

I want to go back to Sandstone and have an experience or two in the Ballroom and I want to have that threesome and I also want to find out how a guy my age who was raised in the same traditions I was raised in could unlearn jealousy enough to share his lady with me and I want to see if I would ever be able to even consider reciprocating and what it all means in the larger scheme of things and whether any of this seems likely to rub off on the world down the hill.

By and large, I think that Sandstone has spoiled me for the world down the hill.

What You Will Get Out of This Article

THIS ARTICLE will tell you what it's like to take the est training and to hang out with Werner Erhard, the founder of est. Reading about my experience is as good as having done it yourself, plus which you will have saved yourself a lot of pain, boredom, and $250.

Now, if you buy that last statement, then perhaps you will also buy it if I told you that last night I met Catherine Deneuve at a party, she invited me back to her suite at the Sherry Netherland, where she proceeded to take off all my clothes and cover me from head to toe with Reddi Wip, then slowly lick off every bit of it—and that my description of this experience would be as satisfying to you as if you had had it yourself.

How I Got Involved with est

How I got involved with est is that one night nearly two years ago—February 21, 1975, to be precise—I allowed myself to be dragged to hear some guy named Werner Erhard speak at the Commodore Hotel in New York. I had no idea who Werner Erhard was or what est was, but I agreed because I figured it would be only an hour or so and then we'd go out to dinner, and that would be fun. I figured Werner Erhard was some old German geezer.

My friend Dory and I arrived at the Commodore and found that about two thousand other people wanted to hear this old German geezer, too, and that everybody had to wear a name tag with his or her first name on it, which pissed me off. I allowed an est volunteer to slap a pressure-sensitive name tag with DAN lettered on it on my sweater, and I went inside. I knew that when I pulled off the name tag it would take some of the nap from my sweater, and that pissed me off even more, and then I went into the ballroom, where this guy Erhard had already started to speak, and I couldn't find the friends I was supposed to meet there or even an empty chair to sit on, and I was so pissed off I didn't hear what Erhard said for the first ten minutes I was there.

Werner Erhard turned out to be neither old nor German, and when I finally started listening to him, I thought that what he was saying was sort of funny, and sort of outrageous, and not a little perverse, which is generally enough to get me to listen awhile. Erhard was doing his by-now-famous shtick about the rat in the laboratory maze, locating a tunnel that contained cheese. If the cheese is withdrawn, Erhard was saying, the rat eventually gets the idea and abandons the tunnel it was in. The difference between rats and people, he said, is that people would rather stay in the cheeseless tunnel, just to prove that they were right to be there.

I was pretty sure that, no matter how good he sounded, Erhard didn't know anything I didn't know after seventy or eighty years of therapy.

"If you're listening to me, you're listening to the wrong person in here," Erhard happened to be saying at that point.

"I came here to get you to listen to *yourself*, not to me. I don't think I know something that if you knew you'd be better off. I think *you* know something that if you *knew* you knew you might be a little better off."

Lots of zealous applause and knowing laughter. I happen to *hate* zealous applause and knowing laughter. I kind of liked what the guy was saying, but not all the zealous agreement he was getting from most of the two thousand people in the audience. I was pretty much turned off by the whole thing.

During the intermission—I now knew that this event was going to run at least three hours—a disagreeable, pushy young man with a close-cropped black beard approached me and Dory and tried very hard to get us to sign up for the est training. Dory was a little more willing to consider it than I was, but when we learned that the training occupied two complete weekends and that we couldn't even get into it till June, we were even more put off. I have a house in East Hampton and, starting in May, I try to get up there every weekend. Nonetheless, for some inexplicable reason, and either *because of* or *in spite of* the persistent nagging of the objectionable young person with the beard, both Dory and I finally decided to give up $250 apiece—and two probably sensational weekends in June at the beach—and we signed up for the est training.

I don't know what Dory's rationale was. Mine was that I could always write about the damned thing if it didn't turn out well and that weekends in East Hampton in June were usually rainy.

The Pretraining Seminar

A COUPLE of days before we were to begin our first est weekend, we attended a pretraining seminar at another hotel. Before we went inside, we had to fill out a questionnaire (we were supposed to have done this at home and mailed it in, but I always save things like that for the last minute) and pay the balance of the $250. I stood in line and had my first contact with the est staff. A middle-aged lady of unspectacular intelligence looked over my filled-out questionnaire and stopped at the place where I hadn't written what I expected to get out of the training. She asked why I was taking the training. It seemed pointless to say I thought Erhard had said some perverse things and that a pushy person with a beard had prodded me, or that it probably rains most weekends in East Hampton in June. I said I didn't know. It was clearly not O.K. with her that I didn't know.

"Look," she said, "you want to improve your life and do better and be happier, don't you?" That seemed safe enough to commit to. I said sure. "Then write that in the space," she said. I did. I put on a name tag and was then allowed into the seminar.

Two hundred and fifty chairs were arranged facing the stage, upon which stood a youngish man named David Norris, who soon revealed himself to be almost as droll and as perverse as Erhard. He told us a little bit about est, how it had graduated forty-three thousand people—the figure is now over ninety-two thousand—in thirteen cities in its four-year existence. He outlined the ground rules of the training—how we were to agree to be in the room from the start to the end of each training day for the four days of the training, not to sit near anyone we knew, not to take a watch into the room, not to take notes or tape-record the training, to abstain from all liquor, pot, uppers, downers, or medications not prescribed by a doctor from the start of the first session till the end of the fourth. There would be two breaks each day to go to the bathroom and one to get some food.

"How long is the food break?" someone asked.

"As long as it takes to eat," Norris replied.

"If we aren't allowed to wear watches, how will we know when to come back?"

"You won't," said Norris pleasantly. "So I suggest you return from your break immediately."

"Will the training room be air-conditioned?" asked somebody else.

"Yes," he replied. "Unless it isn't."

Everything he said he restated and repeated a number of times. I didn't understand why he was being so redundant till I heard people keep asking questions he had already answered several times.

"If I have a headache during the training," said someone who knew better, "can I take an aspirin?"

"If you have a headache during the training, you do not get to take aspirin," said Norris, "you get to have a headache."

"Why do you have that rule?"

"We never explain the rules. Just follow the instructions and take what you get. That's the est koan—follow the instructions and take what you get."

We were told that we would have an opportunity in the training to turn our lives around, to make our lives work, to take responsibility for our lives, to rehabilitate our ability to experience life. Many people stood up to ask pointless, repetitious, or abusive questions. To these, Norris merely answered a cheerful "Thank you for your question."

I had already decided to write about the training, thus, typically, putting myself slightly at a distance from the experience. I had also decided, along with probably most of the people in the room, that I wasn't *necessarily* committing myself to following the rules. Oh, I might follow them if it wasn't too inconvenient or uncomfortable, but, well, rules were made to be broken, right?

There was a short intermission and during it I walked up to the stage and asked Norris if, since I was writing a piece on est for *Playboy*, the no-note-taking rule applied to me. I knew he'd say it applied to me before I asked it, but I asked it anyway. He said it applied to me. At the end of the break, I was interested to see that not only did I start making notes quite openly but I also moved up to one of the front rows, so that Norris could see it too. My hostility to authority was so great that it wasn't enough merely to break the rules, I also had to let the authority who represented the rules know I was breaking them. Interesting.

Norris said we'd encounter three selves within us in the training: The first is the one we *pretend* we are, the second is the one we *fear* we are, and the third is the one we *really* are. He also said that by the end of the training, we'd know the answer to the Zen koan "What is the sound of one hand clapping?"

I wasn't sure I needed to meet my three selves, but I'd always wanted to know the sound of one hand clapping.

The First Day of Training

THE TRAINING is held in a ballroom of the Statler Hilton Hotel. On the first day, Saturday, June 21, 1975, it starts promptly at eight-thirty a.m. I have a few things going on with me about all this. First, I hate getting up at seven a.m. *any* day, particularly a Saturday. Second, the night before is my thirty-ninth birthday, and not only am I not sure whether I want to be thirty-nine, I am positive I don't want to go to bed early, not drink, and do all the other swell things that est suggests.

Dory and I pick up our name tags, put them on, and enter the ballroom. Inside, most of our two-hundred-and-fifty-member group are already seated on chairs facing the stage. Precisely at eight-thirty, a young man with short black hair, slacks, sportscoat, and sport shirt with the collar out ascends to the stage. The young man's name is Michael. He moves like a robot. He has a disquieting gleam in his eye. I fear he is our trainer and that I will have to look at him all weekend.

Michael addresses us in cold, humorless tones, repeats each of the ground rules endlessly and invites those of us who are unwilling to keep them to get the hell out. After at least an hour of such appealing stuff, Michael exchanges places with a tall, similarly dressed guy named Landon Carter, who, it turns out, is to be our trainer.

I want to get very *clear* about something, as they say in est, right now: I am a practicing hetero. I have sex exclusively with ladies, and I am not turned on by the idea of doing it with any guy. But Landon Carter is so good-looking it is almost offensive. He looks like Keir Dullea, except that next to Landon, Keir Dullea would look like Marty Feldman. What's worse, Landon is smart, funny, and handles himself brilliantly onstage for fifteen to eighteen consecutive hours with boundless energy while people in the audience can barely remain sitting upright. O.K., now that we have that out of the way, we can go on.

Landon continues Michael's harangue about the ground rules. Landon calls us assholes. Several people stand and say they object to being called assholes. Unfortunately, every one of them demonstrates himself to be exactly that. Landon says that, although we are assholes, the training is asshole-proof and that we cannot fail to get the result of the training.

The training breaks down into three types of activities. One, the data: The trainer presents an interminable amount of philosophical, semantic, and epistemological material—what Erhard calls "dogshit metaphysics"—frequently outlining it on two large blackboards on the stage. Two, the processes: We close our eyes, "go into our space" and are guided by the trainer through a number of meditative exercises designed to get us in touch with our senses and our experience. Three, the sharing: We are encouraged to ask questions or share our experiences with the group by raising a hand and speaking into a portable microphone. Whenever anyone shares, the rest of us are required to acknowledge him with applause. "Either applaud or throw money" is the lame joke that accompanies this instruction.

I, personally, do not find that going four or five hours at a time without peeing is terribly hard, nor do I fall in a swoon from not being able to eat between eight-thirty a.m. and the only meal break some twelve to fourteen hours later. No, my trouble is headaches. The kind that shatter your skull any time anyone speaks above a whisper. Although there has never been any question of whether I am philosophically willing to break the ground rules and take anything for my headache— I'd sneaked a watch into the training room in my pocket, after all—I do manage to hold out for nearly eight hours before slipping into a broom closet on our second pee break and popping two gorgeous Excedrins into my throat.

Landon shows us a process for getting rid of headaches— of any pain, in fact—wherein we describe the pain precisely, locate its boundaries, decide how much water it could hold if it could hold water, say what color it is, and so on. If you let it, it works. I don't let it. After the meal break, most of us have trouble staying awake, so Landon shows us a process for getting rid of tiredness by precisely describing its symptoms. I don't let this work for me, either.

The first day's training ends at two-forty a.m. I am half frozen from the excessive air conditioning, my buttocks ache from eighteen hours of sitting, and I have a jet-black forty-gallon killer of a pain in my head.

The Second Day

BY THE second day, we are all old hands. We know that Michael will begin each segment of the day by asking if any of us is wearing a watch or sitting next to somebody we know, and so on. We know he will preface each break with the time and with the precise location of the rest rooms, in case any of them has moved. We have gotten to know our group's main characters: a young man with a beard, named Frank, who is brownnosedly enthusiastic over everything Landon says; a funny, fat, middle-aged Jewish lady named Pearl, who is befuddled by everything Landon says; a young woman of average attractiveness named Susan, who keeps saying how beautiful she is and how many celebrities she knows and how European men and European skiing are superior to domestic varieties; a middle-aged Latin named Arch, who blames all his troubles on his bad back and other ailments, a classic victim; a man in his sixties named Marty, who keeps saying his life is perfect and that he has no problems.

On the second day, we learn how we jam things and people into our belief system instead of experiencing them as they really are, that we do this to prove ourselves Right and others Wrong and that we are so committed to proving ourselves Right and others Wrong that we're willing to sacrifice our lives to do so.

The processes on the second day can be done in places other than our chairs. For the first one, most of us lie down on the floor, close our eyes and try to get in touch with some chronic pain or other physical symptom of ours and whatever ancient memories of fear or anger or whatever it dredges up for us. A few minutes into this process, I begin to hear moans and whimpering on all sides of me, then crying, laughing, screaming, shrieking, and sounds of people puking their guts out. It is very surreal, very frightening, like suddenly finding yourself in the middle of an insane asylum. What is going on around me makes it impossible for me to continue doing the process. My sole concern is for my personal safety. I soon realize that I am strong enough to take care of myself whatever happens and that the worst that might occur is that I could get a little puked on.

After what seems like hours, Landon terminates the process, tells us to readjust ourselves to the reality of the room, to open our eyes and sit up. Suddenly, a voice from the middle of the floor screams, "I can't move!"

We are all seated on the floor, and it is impossible to tell who is yelling or what is going on. It develops that who is yelling is old bearded, brownnosing Frank, who is convinced he is paralyzed. Holy Christ, I think to myself, am *I* glad I'm not the trainer here. What the hell happens now?

"I can't move!" screams Frank at Landon.

"Great," says Landon with imperturbable calm. "I got that you can't move."

"You goddamned bastard!" Frank screams. "I'm paralyzed! Don't you care that I might be paralyzed for the rest of my life, you fucking son of a bitch?"

"No," says Landon, "because I'm clear that you will only be paralyzed for as long as you *want* to be paralyzed. So don't run your fucking paralyzed racket on me and expect sympathy, because you won't get any."

Frank yells more obscenities at Landon, but it is clear that Landon is willing for Frank to be paralyzed for the rest of his life, if that is what Frank wants to do to himself, so pretty soon Frank gets unparalyzed. It is a striking illustration to me of what we can do to ourselves to try to make others Wrong. Frank was clearly willing to consider being paralyzed for the rest of his life just to prove Landon Wrong.

We break for dinner at nine p.m. When we come back, we do a process in which we all have a chance to stand on the stage, a few at a time, and do nothing, while everyone else simply stares at us and while a handful of specially selected robotlike est graduates strolls by us, stopping at random to stare at selected trainees. When my group is up on stage, I have the honor of Landon himself walking up to me and spending several minutes or hours—I'm not sure which—trying to stare me down. A lot of people find that this process makes them either burst into tears or begin vomiting. I myself find it oddly easy.

The last process of the night finds most of us lying on the floor again, trying to imagine, first, that the people on all sides of us are terrifying to us, then realizing that *we* are terrifying to *them*. If the process before dinner was notable for insane screaming, crying, and hysterical laughter, this one makes the other look like nursery school. I wonder what mass murders the innocent guests at the Statler Hilton that night think are going on inside our closed ballroom.

The last thing Landon tells us before we complete our first weekend of training at only one a.m. is that, as frightened as we are of the man on the street, be he cop, mugger or what not, he is just as frightened of us. Landon jokingly suggests that during the next week, we try staring down someone walking toward us on the street and, when we are almost upon him, to suddenly yell "Boo!" The training day ends on an incredible high, with people flinging themselves out into the street, yelling "Boo!" at hapless passersby.

The Mid-Training Seminar

IN THE week between the first and second training weekends, we have a Mid-Training Seminar, led by David Norris. Trainees stand and share that they are having the highest highs of their lives, the lowest lows, that they gave up their jobs or got new ones, that they broke up with their mates or found new wonders in their relationships, that they yelled "Boo!" and scared the shit out of lots of mean-looking people.

During this week, I have occasion to phone the est office a number of times, a less than satisfying experience. First, I find it sets my teeth ever so slightly on edge when est staffers answer the phone by saying, "This is So-and-so; how may I assist you?" I have had explained to me the difference between help and assistance, how help implies that the helper is O.K. and the helpee not O.K., whereas assistance has no such emotional charge, but still it sets my teeth on edge. I also find it sets my teeth on edge to be put on hold and disconnected several times in succession, and this seems to be a *spécialité de la maison.*

During this week, I also get a call from a lady named Suzanne Wexler in the Public Information Office of est headquarters in San Francisco. I don't yell "Boo!" at her, but I do decide to be a smartass.

"This is Dan," I say. "How may I assist you?"

Suzanne says that she has heard I am writing an article about est for *Playboy.* I say this is true. She says that at least three other people have told the est office they are writing articles about est for *Playboy.* The old me instantly would have gone on the defensive, said "Well, you could check my editor," and so on and so on. But all I say now is "That's interesting." Perfect. How like a Landon Carter. Suzanne says that est isn't particularly interested in having an article done on it. I say that that is interesting, too. She says that at one time, the est Public Information Office had wanted Werner to be interviewed for the *Playboy Interview,* but that *Playboy* had replied that Werner was neither famous nor infamous enough and that *Playboy* wasn't interested. She asks whether I want to interview Werner for my article. I say sure. She says that Werner might not want to be interviewed by *Playboy* now. "Well," I say, more Landonlike than ever, "either he will or he won't." That seems to throw her.

My God, I think, not only does this est stuff work, it

even works on the est staff. Perhaps it even works on Werner himself!

The Second Weekend

OUR TRAINER for the second weekend is not Landon Carter but a man named Hal Isen. Hal is attractive, slim, dressed in a sportscoat with sport-shirt collar outside the coat, and he also talks and moves a good deal like Werner. I decide that all est trainers are little copies of Werner and should have Werner as a title: Werner-Landon, Werner-Hal, Werner-David, and so on, and that the head man should be called Werner-Werner.

Even though Hal is not Landon, which I hold against him for a while, I soon grudgingly realize that I like Hal not only as much as Landon but more so. He seems to have more of a sense of humor. He seems to be more human. Maybe those are not good qualities in an est trainer, but I respond to them.

The data that Hal gives us is from Werner's training manual, of course, so it's a continuation of what Landon had given us the week before. There are new metaphors: Hal likens the way we conduct our lives to driving a car by steering with the rearview mirror instead of the steering wheel and continually wondering why we have so many accidents. There is the metaphor of the silver box: We treasure our best sex experience inside a figurative silver box and every time we have another sex experience, we take out the one in the silver box to see if the new one was as good. If not, we judge it worthless and discard it. If it was better, we judge the *old* one worthless, discard *it* and put the *new* one in the silver box.

There is a demonstration of how we make decisions and choices based on our considerations and prejudices rather than on the here and now: "Chocolate or vanilla, which do you choose?" "Vanilla." "Why vanilla?" "Because I'm allergic to chocolate." "Then your consideration of being allergic to *chocolate* is what chose vanilla, not you. Chocolate or vanilla, which do you choose?" "Chocolate." "Why chocolate?" "Because I *like* chocolate." "Then your consideration of liking chocolate chose it, not you. Chocolate or vanilla, which one do you choose?" "Chocolate." "Why chocolate?" "Because that's what I chose." "Ah, perfect—you chose chocolate because you chose chocolate. And now, everybody, what is the sound of one hand clapping?" Two hundred and fifty voices respond as one: "The sound of one hand clapping is the sound of one hand clapping." Funny how we hadn't seen that before. Plain as the nose on your face. Plainer.

"The answers they give in the training are like Chinese food," observes a trainee named Betsy. "At first they fill you up, but an hour later you're empty again. That's probably because so much of est is based on Oriental philosophy."

Onstage, Hal is waxing very philosophical. "What would you call a piece of chalk that expands infinitely in all directions?" he asks.

"I'd call it Sir," murmurs a young man on my right.

The sharing now either is more interesting than the first weekend or else we are putting up less resistance to what our fellow trainees are saying. Fat Pearl shares that she's come to the realization she is overeating to punish her husband, who likes skinny ladies. A fat lady named Connie shares that she accidentally called the Statler Hilton the Staten Hitler.

At some point midway into the fourth day, Hal begins speaking about the mind and how it functions. The syntax could be chattier—"The mind is a linear arrangement of multisensory total records of successive moments of Now"—but the sense of it I find brilliant.

"The purpose of the mind," says Hal, "is survival—the survival of the being or of anything that the being considers itself to be." The mind, he says, sees things as either Right or Wrong, Win or Lose, Self-Justification or Invalidation. The mind equates one end of the spectrum with survival, the other end with death. In other words, to be wrong or to lose is the same as death. The mind records early experiences of shocking pain or loss—whether near fatal or merely seemingly near fatal—not as *threats* to survival but as *means* to survival.

In other words, if as a baby, you fell down a flight of stairs and nearly died but somehow survived, this experience got filed in your baby brain under "Ways to Escape Dying," not under "Klutzy and Painful Ways to Spend an Afternoon." Or, to put it another way, if, as a baby, you nearly drowned in a bathtub, then that got filed in your memory bank as a survival experience, and you probably have a history of near drownings.

Or—and as Hal says this, all my deep relationships with women in the past flash before my eyes—*if someone left you and you survived, then you think the way you survive is to have someone leave you.* That ring any bells with any of you out there? It sure as hell does with me.

Now, then, what happens when anything in your present environment is in any way similar to any of these stored, painful, so-called survival experiences is that the entire stack of them floods in on you and has total command over you. This explains why you often see actual grown-ups acting like two-year-olds and accounts for such phenomena as, for example, the General Behavior of People in New York.

Hal goes on to emphasize that when such a stock of experiences takes you over, it literally runs you and you have nothing to say about it, because you are nothing but a machine. You have no choice but to react like an automaton; you are totally at the effect of whatever stimuli are pushing your mechanical buttons.

People in the chairs begin to grumble. Several of them

stand up and object—*they* are not machines. Hal persists: We are all machines, we have no control over our lives, we are nothing but effect, effect, effect, effect, effect. And that, says Hal, grinning wickedly, is the message we have all come here to get. That is what we have each paid $250 to get. Do we get it?

I watch rage well up inside me and in many of those around me. "I got it!" shrieks brownnose Frank and he begins giggling hysterically. All the zealots and brownnosers begin to giggle and say they got it. All the professional cynics like me begin to grumble and swear. I can't believe it—this is the culmination of four days' data and processes? This is the hotshit system that was going to transform our lives?

Hal asks all those who think they've gotten it to stand. They stand, grinning like the assholes I knew they were. "Great," says Hal. "Fabulous." Then he asks all those who *know* they haven't gotten it to stand. These, he says, couldn't be so certain they hadn't gotten it unless they *had* gotten it. Several people furiously try to leave the room. All but one are talked back inside, grumbling.

Now Hal asks all those who don't *know* if they've gotten it to stand. I get up with a raggle-taggle bunch of others and I engage Hal in a fairly drawn-out dialog that consists of my being furious and not being able to show it and of my telling Hal that there is no way I can win the argument since he can always defeat any point I make by defining certain terms to suit his own purposes, and that that is semantics and sophistry. Hal smiles and says I got it.

At length I sit down, not because I'm satisfied, but because I figure I can put all this in my article and point out what a rip-off the est training is.

The last person to sit down is a truculent lady in one of the front rows on the left. The way Hal gets her to sit down is to whisper something in her ear. She giggles and sits down.

A moment later, she raises her hand, stands up, and says, "I've been deaf in one ear all my life. What you whispered to me I just realized was in my deaf ear. I heard it perfectly. I hear perfectly in my deaf ear now. I guess I got it, after all."

The zealots all whoop and cheer. I am even more furious than before. All the rules I have been breaking covertly I now begin breaking right out in the open: I pop Excedrins, take notes, flash my watch, you name it. Curiously, nobody seems to notice.

Being angry makes my headache worse. I try not being angry. If you try not being angry when you're angry, Hal had told us earlier, you are lying and your anger will persist. If you acknowledge your anger, take responsibility for it, *experience* it, it will go away. I acknowledge my anger, take responsibility for it, experience it. My anger goes away. Which makes my headache go away. Which makes me angrier than ever. Which gets my headache back again. I am experiencing what est calls an *upset*.

On the next break, Fat Pearl is growling that she didn't need to spend $250 to learn that she is a machine and that she overeats because she overeats. Dory asks her if that is all she got for her $250. "No," says Fat Pearl, "I learned how to say fuck—fuck fuck fuck fuck fuck. I'm going home and tell my husband not to fuck with me."

The fourth day is over close to five a.m. Near the end, old est graduates come out, and as we pass into another room for our graduation ceremony, they applaud us. If I weren't still so furious, I might have found the experience very moving.

Shortly after five, we are dismissed. The sky is already getting light. Dory and I go to my house, sit out on my roof, drink champagne and orange juice, and watch the sun come up. Since there are no est staffers around, I am free to enjoy myself.

The Post-Training

A FEW DAYS after our second weekend, we go to yet another hotel for our post-training seminar. Hal is the seminar leader and I am appalled to note how glad I am to see him and all the other members of my training group: Fat Pearl, who stands and shares that she's lost three pounds in the three days since the training ended, old stuck-on-herself Susan, even brownnosing old Frank.

Hal invites us to sign up for the first series of graduate seminars, titled "Be Here Now." There are ten seminars in each series and they cost three bucks a night. Est is not making an enormous profit on them. A lot of members of my training group sign up. I do not.

In the next few days, many friends call and ask me how I liked the training. I say it was so-so—a lot of sophistry, a lot of semantics, a lot of boredom. The best parts of it, I tell them, are similar to things I am getting in group therapy anyway, but that Dory seems to have gotten a lot out of the training. She's becoming more assertive, more willing to tell people what she wants from them. Dory really got a lot out of it, I tell them. But not me.

And then a curious thing happens. I hear somebody who hasn't taken the training put it down inaccurately, and I hear myself at first correct him and then go on to say that the training *was* valuable. I actually hear myself say those words. And then, a few days later, it happens again—I actually hear myself defend est. By the time it happens a third time, I am forced to revise my position and, when asked about it, merely say that I thought the training had value.

That is in the beginning of July. In the beginning of August, I go off to East Hampton for six weeks, vowing not to return to New York for any reason till at least mid-September. The est office in San Francisco calls and asks if I still want to interview Werner. I say I do. They say they still don't know if Werner will talk to me but that he may be in New York in a few days, on August 7th, to do a special guest seminar at the Felt Forum and, if he decides to see me, that may be a good opportunity. I say I'm not going back to New York till at least mid-September under any circumstances. They say that Werner probably wouldn't see me, anyway.

A Meeting with Werner Himself

ON AUGUST 7th, regardless of all pronouncements to the contrary, I find myself at the Plaza Hotel in New York, shaking hands with Werner Erhard. Werner is good-looking and beautifully dressed in a tasteful and expensive-looking beige shirt with epaulets and tannish-gold slacks. He looks slightly shorter and pudgier than he seemed from a distance when I saw him at the Commodore.

I have brought along a tape recorder, a note pad and about two dozen questions. I needn't have bothered. Werner is politely defensive, evasive, distrustful of journalists, and talks about what *he* wants to talk about for the hour he has granted me. I've already done some research and learned that Werner Erhard was born in Philadelphia on September 5, 1935, and was baptized John Paul Rosenberg in the Episcopalian Church; his father, Joe, was a convert to Christianity around the time of Werner's birth.

Werner married his high-school girlfriend, Pat, and subsequently had four children with her. In 1960, he left his wife and children and disappeared. On the day he disappeared, he changed his name from Jack Rosenberg to Werner Erhard. "I had a very determined mother and an uncle who was a captain in the police department," says Werner, "so I wanted a name as far from Jack Rosenberg as I could get." He got

Werner Erhard from a combination of names—Werner Heisenberg and Ludwig Erhard—he found in an article on Germany in *Esquire* on the very plane that bore him out of Philadelphia.

Werner married his present wife, Ellen, on the West Coast and had three children with her. They live in Marin County, just north of San Francisco.

As to his skipping out on his wife and children and all the rest of it, Werner says that he has communicated all this information to thousands of people, which is the first step in taking responsibility for something. The second step, he says, is to correct as much of the damage that you've created as can be corrected, and this he has done as well. He has renewed his relationships with his former wife and his kids, his parents, and everyone else he skipped out on—they have all even taken the est training—and the next thing to do, he says, is just to let it be. He is writing a letter to his graduates to communicate where he's at about it, "and from that point on," he says, "I'm going to allow people to say whatever they have to say about my past and let it be. I'm sure I will be accused of everything from being the father of someone's illegitimate child to being a child molester, to being a tax evader, to being a CIA agent."

I ask Werner why he has finally agreed to see me.

"I felt that it was legitimate to spend some time with you since you've been kind enough to take responsibility for taking the training and since the feedback we've gotten about your being in the training was that you participated as a participant rather than stood back as an observer. I felt that that was a contribution to communicating the truth on your part, so it was legitimate for me to make at least some contribution to what you're doing."

All very well, and yet I haven't really gotten anything out of this interview that I've come for, and my hour is now up. I feel frustrated. I tell Werner that the sort of journalism I do has a lot more to do with experience than reporting or interviewing. I tell him about the first piece of journalism I'd ever done, a story in *Life* about firemen. I'd gotten the assignment because I was terrified of fire and wanted to know more about it. To write the piece, I hung out with firemen for five months, riding on the fire trucks and racing into burning buildings with them. It turned out to be a good story, I say, because I was able to experience and communicate what it was like to be a fireman.

Werner looks at me like I have said the magic words. It is as if he were listening to me for the first time. I feel we have finally communicated—for only thirty seconds of the hour, but it is at least a beginning. I tell him I want to talk to him again when he comes back to New York. He says O.K.

Werner at the Felt Forum

THE FELT FORUM that night is packed with thousands of est graduates. Werner is not nearly as impressive as he was the night I saw him at the Commodore and decided to take the training. He speaks for awhile and introduces all seven of his children and has them come up to the stage. He also calls up his mom and dad, his Uncle Al and his Aunt Edith, and kisses them all on the mouth.

About the only thing he says that I consider notable is about my visit with him earlier that day: "A gentleman came up to see me today who is writing an article about me. Actually," says Werner, "he's writing an article about *himself* and I'm just a small part of it." (Actually, *I* had said those very words to Werner at the elevator.) "Actually," says Werner, over the hoots of laughter that greet this statement, "*he* was the one who said that, and I thought it was terrific."

How to Be a Jewish Son

ONE BELIEF I have always held, from the age of seventeen, when I first moved out of my folks' home in Chicago, until the summer of my thirty-ninth birthday, was that I was constitutionally incapable of spending more than three consecutive days in my parents' company. The first day of any visit was always exceedingly pleasant, the second was always pretty nice, too, and by the third I invariably found myself snapping out grouchy, sarcastic replies to their most innocent questions and, in general, behaving like a high-school sophomore. I happen to be very *fond* of my parents, you understand; it's just that I have never been able to spend three consecutive days with them. I figured this was simply an immutable law of the universe, like E equalling mc^2.

Shortly after completing the est training, I invited my parents out to my house in East Hampton for a vacation. I invited them for a week and a half, but what I figured I'd do was spend the first weekend with them, and then on the third day, while I was being transformed into a teenage Mr. Hyde, I would babble something believable about story conferences in New York and split.

And so my folks came out to East Hampton and we spent an exceedingly pleasant first day together and a pretty good second one, and then right on schedule, on day number three, I grew fangs and excess body hair and wanted out. I made my planned excuses about business in New York and then I did a curious thing. Instead of leaving, I went outside into the woods and did a little heavy thinking. I thought about the part in the est training where I learned that I was a machine and that all I could do was react, react, react, react, react. I wondered what would happen if, as the est trainers had suggested, I merely looked at what was happening and attempted to actually experience it through. I decided I had nothing to lose. I went back into the house.

The next thing that happened was that my mother and I had a serious discussion about some table knives. Mother suggested that I had a lot of knives in East Hampton and that I ought to take some of them to New York. I replied that I already *had* enough knives in New York and that were I to take any of those in East Hampton there, I would then have too many knives in *New York*. The old feelings started to well up inside me, but I also saw that I was overreacting to the situation and I was able to get a grip on myself. The discussion about knives continued until finally I burst out laughing and said "Mom, what do I have to do to get out of this discussion?" and my father said, also laughing, "Tell her you'll take the damned knives to New York," and Mom laughed, too, and that was the end of it.

The next incident that occurred had to do with the bizarre fact that although my parents are so self-sufficient in their own home they are able even to do such traditionally un-Jewish things as basic carpentry and electrical repairs, the instant they come to *my* house, they are utterly baffled by such problems as How to Turn On the Overhead Light. I must tell you that a few incidents based on this phenomenon arose in East Hampton, that I again found myself prepared to snarl and bite necks, but that each time, before things got out of hand, I was able to stop and look at what was happening and experience it out, rather than react to it in the automatic way I had always reacted to such things in the past.

I didn't go to New York that night, after all. I stayed for ten days and experienced out every single silly situation and sarcastic teenage overreaction that came up. And, in our final and tenth consecutive evening together, my parents and I had a wonderful dinner together and drank a few glasses of wine, and I was able to tell them for the first time in years that I loved them and was delighted they had come and even more delighted I had stayed, and that I guessed I wouldn't have to limit my visits with them to three days any longer.

I think my therapist, Mildred Newman, gets a lot of credit in the preceding, and so, I think, do I. And so, I'm afraid, does Werner-fucking-Erhard. Far out.

I Get Werner to Experience Me

ON OCTOBER 2, I am granted another audience with Werner at the Plaza Hotel. I have made a point of telling the San Francisco office that seeing Werner for only an hour, as before, is of little or no value to me, but that is all they are willing to give me. I go to the Plaza with neither tape recorder nor note pad, and when I see Werner, I tell him why: An hour is too short for me to do the kind of interview I want, so perhaps we can use the time to get to know each other.

It is as if we have never met. Werner is more defensive about journalists and the press than he was the previous time. "Why should I let you interview me?" he says. "What do I get out of it? Every time I let somebody interview me, I get fucked. They misquote me, they get the most basic facts about me wrong. What assurance do I have that that won't happen with you?"

"None at all," I say. "But if it had been my purpose to fuck you in print, I already have all the input I need to do that. Look, I won't get *paid* any more if I interview you than if I don't; I won't get anything out of trying to spend time with you except, hopefully, a clearer picture of who you are and what you're about. In my training, we were told over and over again that we were assholes because we didn't experience people, we merely jammed them into our belief systems. And yet that's exactly what you're doing with me— you're not experiencing *me*, you're jamming me into your belief system of what a journalist is."

Werner nods his head. Once again I see the flash of communication pass between us. "O.K.," he says, "that sounds valid. Tell me something. Tell me your experience of the training."

I still have a lot of resentment about the training. I tell Werner I feel there were some fairly brilliant things in the training, but there was also a lot of sophistry and a lot of boredom.

"Boredom is a very high state," says Werner.

Werner's sort of side-kick-assistant, Jack Rafferty, comes in and tells him that he has to start dressing for his next appointment. As Werner continues to talk to me, he steps behind a high-backed upholstered chair for modesty's sake and changes from his safari suit to a pair of slacks and a blazer. As he's changing his pants, I think I see a dime falling out of Werner's loafer. I ask what the dime was doing there.

"That's Werner's emergency dime," says Jack.

"Werner's emergency dime?" I say.

"In case he has to make an emergency phone call," says Jack. "See, Werner doesn't carry any money. I take care of all that kind of stuff for him."

Werner comes out from behind his chair and he and I and Jack proceed toward the elevators and then on down to the street. As Jack is getting Werner a cab, I say I want to spend a substantial period of time with Werner the next time I see him. Werner says that the only place he can afford such a luxury is in San Francisco; I say I'll be glad to go to San Francisco, but that I don't want to have to keep starting over from square one each time I see him. Werner says that perhaps I won't have to next time and steps into the cab and says he'll see me when he sees me. I can't help wondering, as Jack and I wave goodbye to Werner's departing cab, how, unless somebody is meeting him at his destination, he is going to pay his cab fare with his emergency dime.

"Be Here Now"

In mid-October, I enroll in the "Be Here Now" graduate seminar series. This series is led not by trainers —who all live near Werner in San Francisco—but by various members of the est staff in New York. Our most frequent group leader is a perverse and amusingly outrageous young man whose name is Marvin.

Marvin repeatedly badgers us about bringing guests to the seminars, so that the est staff can have a shot at enrolling them in the training. Most of us graduates bitterly resent being badgered about bringing guests and say so. Mostly, we are told that the resentment is *our* problem, not est's.

Much of the "Be Here Now" series is about handling upsets. The upset I use most frequently in the processes they give us is my irritation at est for badgering us to bring guests.

Nobody Doesn't Like Sara Lee

The "Be Here Now" seminars start promptly at seven-fifteen p.m. If you get there late, you have to go through a little ritual at the door that goes like this: The est volunteer at the door asks you if you're late. You say you are. The est volunteer asks if you have broken your agreement to be there on time. You say yes. The est volunteer asks you if you take responsibility for breaking your agreement. You say yes. The est volunteer asks you if you are willing to re-create your agreement to be on time. You say yes and the est volunteer opens the door and lets you in.

One night, I get to my "Be Here Now" seminar at seven-thirteen and find the door to the seminar room already closed, with a plastic est volunteer guarding the door, with a plastic smile on her face. If you think airline stewardesses are robots, you should see some of the beauties they have at est—they make airline stewardesses look like Sicilians at a wedding. The name tag on this particular robot's chest says she is Sara Lee.

"Are you late?" says Sara Lee. I say I'm not—my agreement was to be there at seven-fifteen and it's only seven-thirteen. "Are you late?" says Sara Lee. I say no, I'm not late, but if she continues asking assholic questions, I *will* be late. "Are you late?" says Sara Lee. I feel tension building up in my forehead. I feel my heart begin pounding in my chest. And then a curious thing happens to me: I realize in a blinding flash of ineffable Zen clarity that I am perfectly willing to stand here the rest of the night, possibly work myself up to an ulcer or a heart attack, simply because I am Right and I have to stick to my position and prove that a mindless assholic robot named Sara Lee is Wrong. (And I sneered at brownnose Frank in the training for his willingness to be paralyzed in order to prove Landon Wrong?)

Clearly, if I am willing to drop the entire *issue* of who's Right and who's Wrong, even though I *know* I'm Right, then I can get on with my life. It isn't fair that I should have to say I am late when I'm not, but then, as they told us in the training, whoever said that life was fair?

"Are you late?" says Sara Lee.

"Fuck yes," I say. "I'm late."

San Francisco

AT JUST about every est function I have ever attended, there is one trainer in the room and a whole lot of trainees or graduates. But this afternoon, I am in a room in San Francisco filled with all nine est trainers and seven trainer candidates and Werner himself, and the only non-trainer in the room is me. It's a curious feeling.

What we are doing is eating a lunch of cold chicken in aspic, and I can't get over how normal-looking and normal-sounding these est trainers are compared with the way I experienced them in my training. There's gorgeous old Landon and dynamic Hal and several others I've seen doing their supercharged est shtick, and here they all are, shoving cold chicken into their cheeks, just like regular people, and talking without theatrics in a normal tone of voice.

A cherished belief of most people—myself included—about the est trainers is that they are all carbon copies of Werner and that they all look alike. Looking at them in a group, this concept is tough to hang on to, since they don't really look alike at all—one has a beard, and one is black, and three are women, and so on. Too bad. I really loved the concept of their all being little Werners.

The trainers and trainer candidates are a pretty high-powered group. Not only are they able to stand on a platform for fifteen to twenty hours every Saturday and Sunday and put on an act that any entertainer would envy, but most of them gave up fairly prestigious careers in academe or medicine or psychology to work for Werner. As a matter of fact, eight people on the est staff have doctorates, three have M.D.s (one of these is a psychiatrist), and six have doctor-of-jurisprudence degrees.

Suzanne Wexler, the nice PR lady I was mean to on the phone, shepherds me around during my San Francisco stay and introduces me to various members of the est staff, including est president Don Cox, who is a former Coca-Cola exec and Harvard Business School professor, and John Poppy, who is a former editor of *Look* and *Saturday Review* and a very sweet man indeed. Most est staffers I see wear the ubiquitous est name tags. All est staffers are theoretically on call twenty-four hours a day and are sometimes awakened in the middle of the night by a seemingly never-sleeping Werner to clarify some vital issue that couldn't have waited till morning.

Most of est's staff had been working in the small cheery office building where I had lunch. But est has now leased a substantial portion of a gigantic old building that looks like the U.S. Treasury, and this building will become est Central, controlling est's national and international activities. The est Public Information Office has already moved into the new old building. Near the door of the Public Information Office, I note a Big Brotherly sign to the effect that all staff members must, upon signing out, leave word where they can be reached, or else "contribute" five dollars.

I find the slavish devotion of the staff to Werner and his apparent insistence upon same to be vaguely unsettling. And I do not at all understand est staffers' eagerness to volunteer so much of their time to work for Werner without further remuneration. Indeed, this eagerness reaches such absurd proportions that I have heard rumors that staffers are fined $100 a day every time they work more than six days a week for est!

Such zealousness seems greatly at odds with the increased independence and heightened feelings of self-worth that most est graduates report as a result of the training. Commenting on this apparent dichotomy, former est trainer Stewart Emergy wryly observes in the December 15, 1975, issue of the Boston *East West Journal*: "The purpose of est is to serve people. The purpose of the est staff is to serve Werner."

That night, I again find myself eating with Werner, this time not in the small bright office building on Union Street but in Werner's dark, tastefully restored Victorian mansion on Franklin Street. The fare is not cold chicken but chilled glasses of kir, endive stuffed with cucumber and dill, salmon in pastry, rice with mushrooms. The table is piled high with fresh ferns and flowers, and the meal is served in the softly lit room by two est staff members dressed as a butler and a maid, both wearing name tags. Present at the table with me and Werner are Bob, Jim, Ernie, and Bernie, who are all professors at Stanford.

After dinner, we adjourn to the living room to hear tapes of Richard Pryor, in the midst of which the staff member who serves as butler materializes to say: "Werner, it's ten o'clock. Your next appointment is ten-thirty." I don't remember ever being at someone's home for dinner when he excused himself for another appointment, but then, I've never been to Werner's for dinner before. Werner bids us farewell, tells me and the Stanford professors we're free to tarry as long as we like, and then moves on to his next appointment.

The following day, Werner has promised me a lunch with just the two of us, during which I'll be able to ask him all the questions I never finished asking him in New York.

Lunch is on an upper floor of the mansion. I am served Campari and Calistoga Water without having been asked what I wanted to drink, just as the previous night we had all been served glasses of kir without being asked. When the food comes, I begin my interview.

"Werner," I say, "why is the attitude of the trainers so tough, so militaristic?"

"It's not militaristic," says Werner.

"O.K., then, tough. People say fascistic. People say Nazi."

"It's neither fascistic, militaristic, Nazi, nor any of those things. It *is* . . . very one-way. It's very what you might call unsympathetic. And the reason behind that is that we're trying to create a situation in which people can learn something from their own way of being. Now, if you do A, and I do B when you do A, if you switch to C and then I switch to D, you don't know where the fuck you're at. But if, no matter what you do, I'm doing A, you *always* know where you're at. It's always you, it's never me. That's why I tell people that my guru is gravity. Or the physical universe. See, you can't move the physical universe. It doesn't give a fuck. Now, is the physical universe fascistic? Is it militaristic? No. It's simply the way it is."

"Specifically," I say, "people make reference to why the trainers call the trainees assholes, why they yell at them, and so on. There is a very definite attitude taken."

"Now, that's a very different story," says Werner. "The purpose of that is to engage people. We don't want people to go through the training as observers, Dan. We don't want them to go through the training in their heads. We want them to go through the training experientially. And so it's important, then, to engage people. And the way you engage people is you tell them the truth. That always engages them. Particularly that thing which they've been trying to hide. And the one thing everybody's trying to avoid is being an asshole. I mean, people are actively trying to avoid that."

"So, by calling them assholes, you're forcing them to confront what they've been trying to hide?" I say.

"Mmmmmm."

"There are a great many rumors about est and Nazi things," I say. "That est graduates greet one another with a Nazi salute, and so on. Where do you think such rumors come from?"

"There is actually a whole Nazi drama in people's heads. That Nazism didn't happen outside us, it happened inside us."

"How do you mean?"

"That it was a function of something we all carry around in us and—"

"Latent sadomasochism or what?" I say.

"That's a little too Freudian for me," says Werner.

"It's my own feeling that people are naturally suspicious and afraid," I say, "and also that nobody quite knows how to deal with the whole Nazi thing. And the combination of your name being Werner Erhard and the fact that the training is so tough, I think, brings out people's ambivalence about it: their fascination for it, the horror of it, the—"

"The whole drama of it. I agree totally," says Werner. "Yeah, if Outward Bound were headed by a guy whose name was Werner Erhard, they'd have the same concern, perhaps. By the way, Dan, the harshness in the training, if I can call it that, has a similar purpose to Outward Bound's purpose of putting you out in the wilderness."

"Which is what?" I say.

"Which is that you've got a stable thing against which to match yourself. And it's a thing that is tough enough so that you can't bullshit it. You know, it's very hard to bullshit a ten-mile hike. First off, it doesn't give a shit. No matter what you say to it, it doesn't care. So you have to listen to your own bullshit when you're talking to it."

"Could you tell me in very brief terms how you hope est could transform society?" I say. "In one sentence, if possible."

Werner laughs at the notion of trying to sum it all up in one sentence, then wonders if it might be possible. "By making it all right for people to tell the truth to themselves about themselves," he says at last.

"Do you think—"

"That wasn't bad, was it?" he says.

"No, it was very nice," I say. "Werner, has it occurred to you that in a couple years' time, there'll be so many est graduates they could constitute a political bloc? And, if so, what could be done about that? Could it be a political party, could it be an instrument for effecting social change?"

"Yeah, it could be all those things. And, mostly that

would be a mistake. I expect est to have an enormous impact on politics, but not as a political thing."

"As an influence in telling the truth?" I say.

"Yes. Let me give you an example. There was a man in Honolulu who, at the time he took the training, was head of the social-welfare program in the state of Hawaii: the prisons, the welfare programs, whatever. And the program he had put together was presented to the legislature and it failed in the legislature in the week between the two weekends of the training. He made a public statement to the press that the program had failed in the legislature, not because the legislature was crappy but because he had not done a good enough job in presenting it. The press was flabbergasted. They literally said they didn't know what to do if politicians were going to start telling the truth. That's the kind of political influence I'd like to see est have."

"Why is the training sold so hard?" I say. "Do the staff members get some kind of commission or cash incentive?"

"There is no incentive other than their own personal incentive to do any of this. They are definitely told if a person says he's not interested in taking the training to immediately terminate the thing."

An est staffer comes in and hands Werner a memo. Werner reads it and gets visibly agitated.

"Do you know what it just cost us for me to read this memo, Locke?" says Werner. "You could have had somebody else make the decision and do it *wrong* and it would've taken less of my time and cost less. You could have let the *dog* decide this—you could have given this decision to the *dog.*"

Locke withdraws apologetically. As he leaves, Werner's dog, Rogue, having perhaps heard he was needed, trots into the room. But Locke doesn't ask Rogue to decide anything, and neither does Werner.

"There is a rumor about," I say, "that your lawyer, Harry

Margolis, is sending money to a secret bank account in the Caribbean and that he's been indicted on tax evasion. I wonder if you'd set me straight on that."

"There's no secret bank account in the Caribbean," says Werner. "What happened was that the Justice Department, through the grand jury system, indicted Harry for conspiracy to make false statements on tax returns."

"For the tax returns of his clients?" I say.

"Yes. And one of the clients mentioned was us. We were not mentioned as co-conspirators. We were mentioned in there merely because our tax return was one of the tax returns on which the Government alleges there was a conspiracy involving Harry and other people to make knowingly false statements. Now, the Government's indictment, when it finally came to be presented in court, was so inaccurate that the Government had to ask to withdraw it, which the court allowed it to do and allowed it to present another indictment."

"But was est ever found guilty of any improper procedures?" I say.

"Est wasn't even *charged* with any improper procedures, let alone found guilty," says Werner.

"The other rumor is that Jesse Kornbluth says that you threatened to kill someone."

"What actually happened was that I used to live in an apartment complex in Sausalito that was on the bay. What you did was to drive into the parking lot there, and in one place in the parking lot, there was an elevator. One night, somebody drove me home. They pulled up in front of the elevator, and we were sitting there talking until I got out to leave. The guy who guards the lot shined his spotlight in the windows of the car. I got out of the car and walked over to him and said, 'Look, I live here. I actually pay rent to park my car here and to drive up and get out and all that stuff, and I would appreciate it, if you want something from me, if you don't shine your light in my eyes but just come over and ask me whatever you want.' I said, 'Don't forget that.'

"A couple of weeks later, somebody drove me home again—it was Gonneke, who's been working for me since before est, you met her—and we were parked in front of the same place. She had her lights on, because I was about to get out of the car, and the guy shined his spotlight in our eyes again. So this time, I got out of the car and walked over to his car and said, 'Get out of the car.' He began to roll the window up. So I opened the car door, reached inside, put my hand around his arm like this, at which point he turned the red flashing light on top of his car on and began to lay on the horn. So I pulled him the rest of the way out of the car, and as I did, he stood up. I grabbed him by the lapels like this and picked him up off the ground a little bit, and I said, 'I told you the *last* time you did that never to do that again, that if you wanted to talk to me, you should come over to talk to me. Now, if you do it again, I'm going to throw you over the fucking embankment.' Which was about three stories down, by the way.

"And he reached down like this, and I assumed he had a gun. I said, 'And if you pull that gun out, I'm going to shove it down your throat.' By that time, Gonneke had pulled off to the side and parked the car, so I put the guy down and that was the end of that. I told Gonneke to go home.

"I went down to the apartment. A knock came at the door and there were two policemen with this guy. They said, 'He wants to make a citizen's arrest for assault and battery.' So I got dressed and we drove down to the Sausalito Police Department. They talked to the man and told him he might be subject to a suit for false arrest if he pressed this assault-and-battery thing and maybe he should reduce it to battery. So he did. I went and got fingerprinted, and so on, and by that time the bail bondsman posted bail for me and we left. I hired an attorney, and the attorney talked to the district attorney, and they agreed that if I was willing to plead guilty to disturbing the peace, that would suffice for them, they wouldn't have a trial, and all that shit. In my naïveté, I agreed to that."

"Why do you say in your naïveté?" I ask.

"Well, because the thing was a definite overreaction, Dan, and it never would've stood up in trial. First, I didn't hit the guy and—"

"Did he have a gun?" I ask.

"I don't know. He had *something* he was reaching for."

"It might have been a mint to freshen his breath," I say.

"Whatever it was, he decided not to reach for it, because he didn't want it shoved down his throat," says Werner. "I have mentioned that incident in public, by the way. Jesse didn't discover that incident. As a matter of fact, there's nothing that has been in the press so far that I haven't mentioned in public—in front of hundreds of people in some cases and thousands of people in other cases. And I've spoken about that incident a couple of times. It never occurred to me that there was anything to report about it. Now I'm a little wiser, so I know that if my *shorts* are striped, that's a matter to be reported on."

Jesse's Article

AN ARTICLE by Jesse Kornbluth appeared in the March 19, 1976, issue of *New Times*. There were a lot of disturbing things in it, such as an explanation of est's tax-shelter setup, which involved Werner's selling the est data to a foreign company, which then licensed it to Erhard Seminars Training in a complicated manner; such as the matters of the fight with the security guard and of Harry Margolis' indictment, which I'd already discussed with Werner; such as the assertion that est hired a private detective to pose as a reporter and reinterview one of the sources of the article; and such as various accounts of Werner's seemingly dictatorial control of the professional and personal lives of those who work for him.

Even though I expected the Kornbluth piece to be a kill piece, even though I knew it had been written as a deliberate hatchet job, it still succeeded in shaking me up. If all Kornbluth said was true, then maybe I was a sucker for finding value in est, for finding Werner himself personally likable. If Kornbluth was right, I had been badly conned.

On Thursday, March 18, I was asked by a TV program in New York called *Midday Live* to appear opposite Jesse Kornbluth. Kornbluth was, of course, taking the anti-est position. I was being asked to take the pro-est position. I resented being placed in the role of est's public defender when I had so many reservations about est myself. I would have preferred to kid it instead—est is easy to kid. But I felt that, despite my own reservations and Kornbluth's allegations, I had gotten definite value out of the est training, and I felt that it was necessary for me to point it out whenever I felt est was being criticized unfairly.

It was a strange debate. Kornbluth, the anti-est person, acknowledged on camera that he had really found the est training itself valuable. I, the pro-est person, acknowledged all my reservations about the organization. As I say, a strange debate.

The following night, Friday, March 19, est invited all est graduates who were in the media to a special seminar in New York that would give us an opportunity to talk to Werner about any number of things, including the Kornbluth article.

The Media Seminar

To THE surprise of absolutely nobody, nearly all questions put to Werner by the more than two hundred est graduates at the media seminar had to do with charges raised in the Kornbluth article. Questioned about est's financial structure, Werner painstakingly described est's legal status as an ultimately tax-exempt charitable trust based in the British Isles. To snide comments about this being an elaborate form of tax evasion, Werner replied that est pays the taxes appropriate to its income and further observed: "I dare say that there is not a person in this room—there might be one or two exceptions—who does not pay as little taxes as he can possibly pay."

When pressed by a persistent questioner who implied Werner was guilty of improper conduct because of the Margolis indictment, Werner temporarily blew his cool: "How *dare* you attack my integrity with guilt by association?" he replied. "Look, if you're trying to make me Wrong, *I* know how to make me Wrong much better than you could *ever* hope to do it. And I'm totally willing to do it: I have done evil things. Leaving a wife and four children is one *hell* of a lot more evil than any of the bullshit that comes up in any of the articles. There is not one fact that is in any way generally considered by people to be evil that I have not shared publicly. Not one.

"Look," said Werner wearily, "it's perfectly all right for people to be suspicious of me and for people to be suspicious of est. If I couldn't stand the heat, I wouldn't be in the *kitchen*, kids.

"The problem is, people think I pretend that I'm doing this out of a love of mankind and that I'm *really* doing it out of a love of money. If I said, 'Look, what I mainly wanted was your $250'—it just so happens I'm smart enough to give you that much in return—you'd love it. You sure would. And it would be a lie. I'm sorry. Because I don't think *you* happen to work for money, either.

"You think if someone gave you all the money in the world, you'd go to a desert island or you'd get two broads and go to Florida. You would like *hell*. You'd go back to work. And if you *really* got your shit together and you had no fears about anything and were totally secure, what you'd do is find a way to contribute to people's lives. Now, *I know that's impossible to believe*. I *know* it. And I know that the things Jesse said make you *crazy*. Look, I'm aware of all that—goddamn it, I'm the guy who put that *training* together, don't you remember?"

A Final Note

IT IS now nearly two years since I first heard Werner Erhard speak at the Commodore Hotel. Werner's hair is shorter now, and he has taken to dropping in on trainings and seminars unannounced and saying things like est will go on, even if it's called something else and even if it's without him.

Two friends of mine took the training recently and were surprised to hear their trainer, Randy McNamara, say that up till a short time ago, est was an evil organization because it was dedicated to its own survival. That has changed, said McNamara, and now, unlike most organizations, est is solely dedicated to serving people. Werner has issued a four-hour taped message to est staffers on this theme and I have already seen some of the repercussions. At an excellent graduate series called "About Sex," which I attended, the pitch to bring guests was softened almost to a whisper. The frequent calls that est graduates used to get from the office, asking if one would like to assist at est functions or in the office, have almost stopped.

Fear of Werner and of est continues to run high among people I know who have not taken the training, however. And when they ask me how I can possibly have anything good to say about either est or Werner, I tell them, as dopey as it sounds, that all I know is my own experience, and that my experience of the est training was that it was valuable, and that my experience of Werner is of a likable man who seems to believe in what he has created. By the time this appears in print, it may be revealed that Werner buys his underwear from Frederick's of Hollywood or that he has romantic interludes with Lhaso Apsos, but, even so, that still won't retroactively make the training I took invalid. And that is absolutely all I have to say about est and Werner Erhard.

Now, then. Let me tell you about that session with Reddi Wip and Catherine Deneuve.